SHIPS THROUGH HISTORY

Ralph T. Ward

SHIPS THROUGH HISTORY

Illustrated by

Samuel F. Manning

THE BOBBS-MERRILL COMPANY, INC.

INDIANAPOLIS   NEW YORK

To Dr. James C. Silvan

THE BOBBS-MERRILL COMPANY, INC.

PUBLISHERS   INDIANAPOLIS   NEW YORK

TEXT COPYRIGHT © 1973 BY RALPH T. WARD
ILLUSTRATIONS COPYRIGHT © 1973 BY SAMUEL F. MANNING
DESIGN BY JACK JAGET
PRINTED IN THE UNITED STATES OF AMERICA
ALL RIGHTS RESERVED
ISBN-0-672-51663-2
LIBRARY OF CONGRESS CATALOG CARD NUMBER: 72-75895
0 9 8 7 6 5 4 3 2 1

Contents

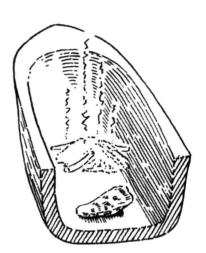

SHIPS THROUGH HISTORY

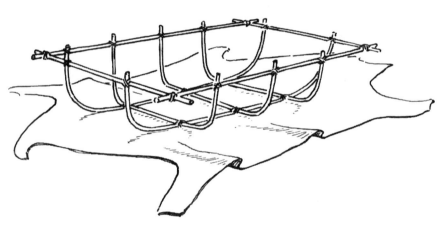

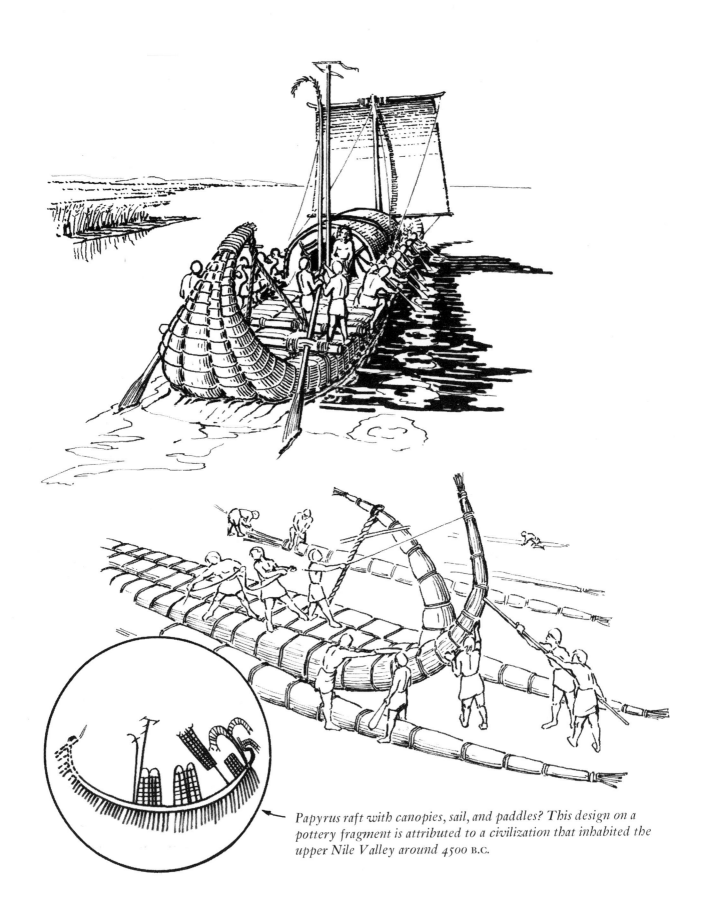

Papyrus raft with canopies, sail, and paddles? This design on a pottery fragment is attributed to a civilization that inhabited the upper Nile Valley around 4500 B.C.

1.
The Mystery of
Ancient Sailing Ships

NO ONE knows who first thought of the sail. The first drawings of boats with sails, dating back to the Egypt of thousands of years ago, show vessels with high curving stem and stern, the mast, holding up the square sail, built like a flagpole. These simple craft look very much like the papyrus boats still being used on the Nile. From Egyptian tombs and buildings of a few hundred years later we find carvings and paintings of a more complex type of sailing vessel, with a double-footed mast that is shaped like a long, narrow "A" and is held steady by ropes attached to it called stays, one tied to the stem and others to the stern. Men on the platformlike stern guide the boat with steering paddles, and the crewmen sit facing forward toward the prow, their paddles drawn up. The wind billows out the long rectangular sail. From this we can tell that the boat is going up the Nile, because the wind that blows through the enclosed Nile Valley all year blows toward the heart of Africa. On their return trip down the Nile toward the Mediterranean, Egyptian boats glide along without sail, carried by the river's current.

Years pass and the pictures change, but you will have to look sharply to catch the difference, for these ships are similar to earlier ones. But now you will notice that the crew sits facing the stern, or the rear of the boat. The difference is important, because it means that the crewmen are rowing instead of paddling. Men using oars to row can propel a larger and heavier boat, for an oar braced on the boat has a great mechanical advantage over a paddle held in the hands.

These boats were made of wood. A Greek tourist in Egypt in ancient times stopped to watch and report on the building of one of these boats. He wrote that acacia wood was generally used, since it was the most plentiful. It was cut into pieces about three feet long which were placed edge to edge and fastened together with pegs to make the shell, or hull, of the boat. Then the timbers, called beams, that ran from one side of the boat to the other were fitted across. The sail was made of papyrus, a paperlike material made from the pithy stems of the papyrus reed laid in layers.

Nile River boats, 3400–3000 B.C. From Egyptian wall reliefs.

The visitor saw many of these acacia boats on the Nile. Some carried a great deal of cargo, for virtually all the cities of Egypt were located on or near the river, and there was continual trading among them. The early Egyptians had no coined money. They did not buy and sell, but exchanged goods by barter. Even the taxes due the Pharaoh were paid with merchandise: the potter gave pots, the cabinetmaker cabinets; and these goods went to the Pharaoh by boat.

Building boats by piecing together the short and narrow cuttings from the scrubby local trees such as acacia, sycamore, fig, tamarisk and willow was an art. However, the genius of Egyptian shipwrights was also reflected in the ships they built of cedar, cypress, fir, and pine. These woods were imported from Syria, and great timber fleets voyaged between Egypt and the Syrian coast year in and year out. But even the ships made from these costly imported woods had hulls without ribs or a keel. (The keel is the heavy bottom timber of a ship on which the rest of the hull is built up.) Without a keel and ribs a ship's hull is weak. To stiffen their ships the Egyptians ran a thick rope the full length of the vessel and fastened it around both ends. This not only added strength but also prevented the ends from drooping.

When Hat-shepsūt was queen of Egypt over three thousand years ago, shipbuilding was already well advanced; nearly all the important general features of the sailing ships used in the Mediterranean for thousands of years after could be found on Egyptian vessels at this time. The queen's ships are shown in reliefs that are quite detailed and lifelike; sailors walk on the yards and pull at the great oars.

The vessels were double-ended: that is, the prow and stern were similar, as in a canoe; but the prow projected out like a ram and was curved only on the inside, while the stern was a complete curve. These seagoing ships were decked, and some of the beams supporting the deck appear to be more than a foot wide.

A single pole mast, situated amidships, replaced the earlier A-frame mast that had been placed forward toward the prow. The sail was square. However, sails were used only when the wind was blowing from behind the ship. If the sail was turned to catch the wind coming from either side, the ship would simply be pushed in that direction, since it had neither a keel nor a strong sternpost rudder. Thus, to sail ahead, the shallow, round-bottomed Egyptian ships could utilize only the aft, or following, wind. When the wind did not blow from behind, out came the oars.

Inscriptions on the reliefs tell us that these ships voyaged to Punt. It is not certain where Punt was, but according to the Egyptians a round trip covered eight thousand miles. In those days such long trips were rarely undertaken, for the ships were propelled in good part by oars.

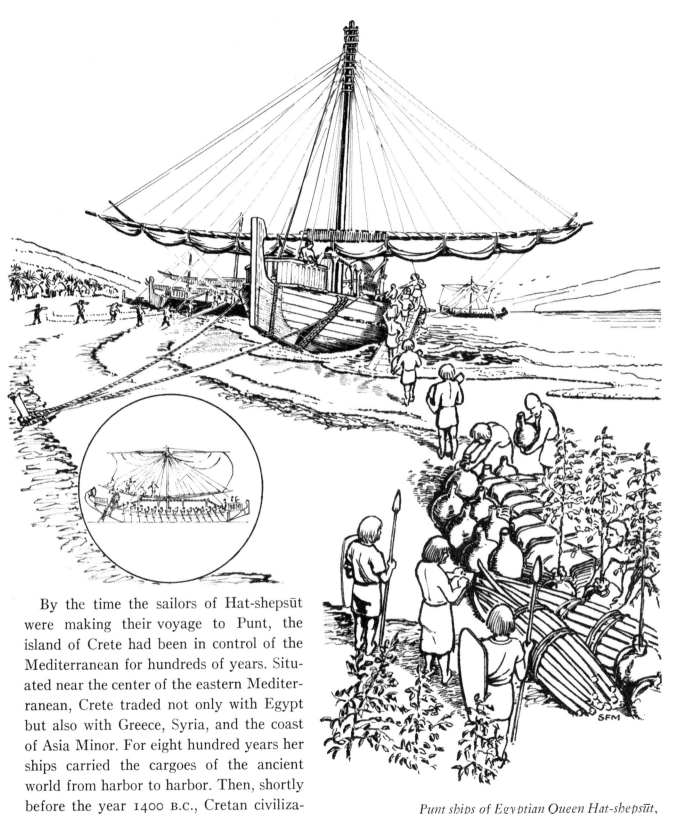

By the time the sailors of Hat-shepsūt were making their voyage to Punt, the island of Crete had been in control of the Mediterranean for hundreds of years. Situated near the center of the eastern Mediterranean, Crete traded not only with Egypt but also with Greece, Syria, and the coast of Asia Minor. For eight hundred years her ships carried the cargoes of the ancient world from harbor to harbor. Then, shortly before the year 1400 B.C., Cretan civilization mysteriously disappeared.

Punt ships of Egyptian Queen Hat-shepsūt, 1500 B.C.

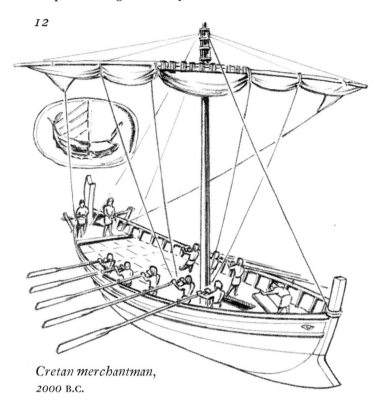

Cretan merchantman,
2000 B.C.

Although Crete was the first great sea-power in the Mediterranean and her people were highly cultured, all we know about Cretan ships comes from pictures so small the details are not really clear. Miniature figures of ships were engraved on round and three-sided stones or gems which were used as seals to stamp clay tablets. These small engravings show ships with both sail and oars, and hulls that have a sharply curved prow and stern. On many of the ships a ramlike projection juts out in front. The evidence available does not indicate whether Cretan ships had a keel. Curiously, on a few of the seals there are ships with two and even three masts, each carrying a sail, yet ships with more than one mast and sail were not common until hundreds of years later. Why these ships were built and how they were used is another Cretan mystery.

With the disappearance of Crete, the Phoenicians, a Semitic people, became the principal traders on the Mediterranean. Phoenicia was a small country on the eastern coast of the Mediterranean that was so narrow all of its cities were ports. Two of them, Tyre and Sidon, located in present-day Lebanon, were famous for their wealth. The Phoenicians traded far and wide, and their glass, dye (the famous Phoenician purple), textiles, and metalwork were in great demand in the ancient world.

Besides being the greatest traders of their day, the Phoenicians were the greatest navigators and colonizers before the Greeks. They had settlements in North Africa and on the Atlantic coast of Spain. Some of the voyages they made are astonishing. On one that took place about 600 B.C. a Phoenician ship sailed into the Red Sea, down the east coast of Africa, around the Cape of Good Hope, and then came back into the Mediterranean through the Straits of Gibraltar: an expedition that took almost three years and covered 16,000 miles.

The Phoenicians had a great fleet of seaworthy ships. In the Bible the prophet Ezekiel gives an interesting description of them: the boards were made of fir, the

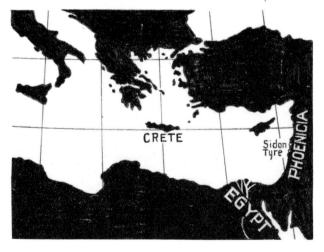

masts of cedar, the oars of oak. The sails were of fine linen from Egypt. Ezekiel also mentions the strength of the Phoenician rowers. That was important, for the wind does not blow so steadily at sea as it does in the Nile Valley.

Taking long voyages in such rough waters as the Atlantic called for strong hulls on Phoenician ships. Paintings in Egyptian tombs show Phoenician merchant ships that resemble Egyptian ships, except they have no rope supports for the hull. This indicates that Phoenician ships were the first ever built with a keel and ribs. They were round-looking, with gently curved prow and stern. A Greek historian visited one of these cargo ships and, being curious about the number of times the captain inspected the ship, asked him about it. "Stranger," the captain said, "before sailing I make sure everything is shipshape. You can't worry about what's not aboard when a storm hits. Besides, there's no time in a storm to stow things as they should have been stowed from the beginning of the voyage." The captain's sensible answer explains why Phoenician seamen were hired by all the great nations of the ancient world.

Phoenicians also used small cargo ships. These can be seen in the sculptured reliefs carved by Phoenician artists that decorated various ancient palaces. They are pictured

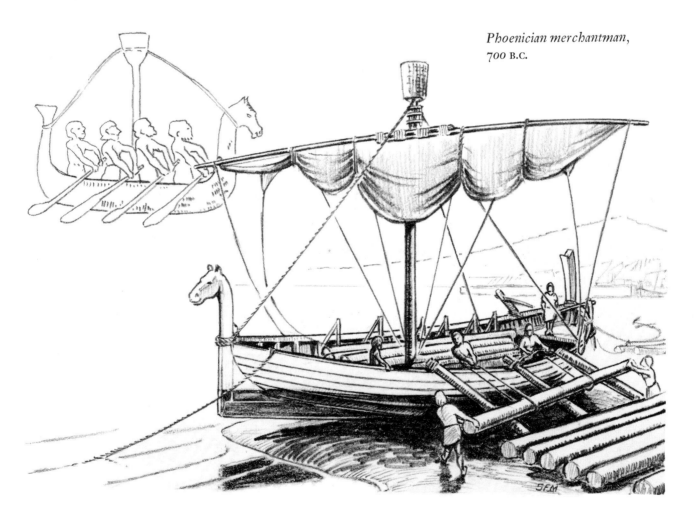

Phoenician merchantman, 700 B.C.

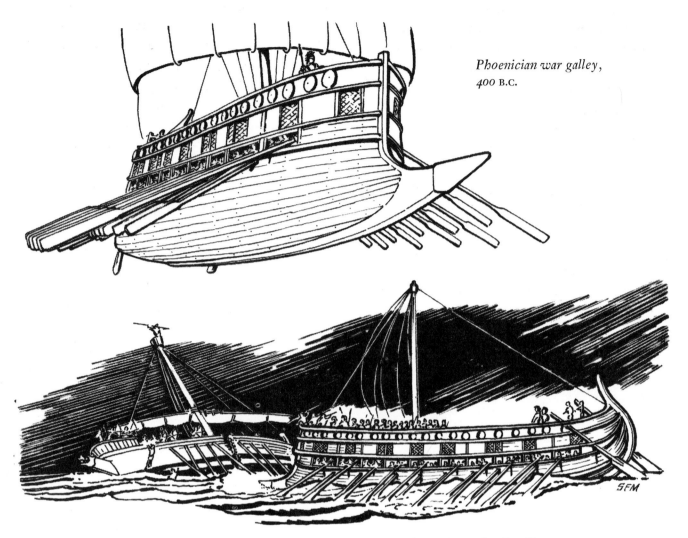

*Phoenician war galley,
400 B.C.*

as being round-hulled, with stem and stern curving upward. Some had sail; others had one row of oarsmen; still others had—and this was something new in shipbuilding—two rows of oars on each side. Small cargo ships under sail or oar power were used both as troop transports and in the lumber trade. King Solomon sent to Phoenicia for lumber, and the Phoenician king, Hiram, wrote to Solomon, saying: "I'll do what you ask about the timber of cedar and fir. My men will bring it down from the forest to the sea. Then I'll have it floated in the sea to whatever place you suggest." Moving timber by floating it is a method still in use. In the

U.S. today, along the Pacific coast, tugs tow log rafts from the Columbia River in Washington to towns in California.

The Phoenicians also built warships—rarely for their own use, since Phoenicia was never a strong military power, but to sell to other countries. These warships were long and narrow, with a pointed prow and high-rising stern. Like the small troopships, they had two levels of oars on each side. From the evidence available it seems that the Phoenicians were the first to experiment with what was to be one of the toughest shipbuilding problems for hundreds of years—how to place oars on a warship to achieve the greatest possible fighting power.

Phoenician ships not only carried purple robes and gold and silver jewelry; they also carried a more valuable gift to other countries—the alphabet. Realizing how useful a written record would be for their trading accounts, the Phoenicians experimented with ways of putting down signs to represent sounds. They evolved a list of twenty-two, beginning with *alaph* and *beth*, from which our word "alphabet" comes. Our modern alphabet developed later when the Greeks, using the Phoenician signs, added a few letters of their own.

As time passed, Phoenician shipping was eclipsed by the Greeks, whose ships then dominated the commerce of the eastern Mediterranean and the Black Sea for more than five hundred years. The docks of Athens and Corinth were stacked high with large jars of wine and olive oil, with works of art and beautiful Grecian pottery to be exported. Greek ships returning from the Black Sea and Asia brought food, lumber, hides, and textiles. Food was in great de-

mand by the large Greek cities, for the land surrounding them was not suitable for growing grain.

The common Greek cargo ship coming from Asia was a single-masted ship called a "round" ship. Its hull was wide and curved upward at the stern. The prow was slightly curved above the rounded hull. There was a raised bulwark (the woodwork running along the sides above the level of the deck). At the stern were two large rudder oars, one on each side. Round ships traveled under sail and sometimes carried as much as 100 to 150 tons of cargo.

In those days anyone voyaging on the sea was in real danger of being captured by pirates and sold into slavery. To meet this threat, vessels were developed that were a combination of trading ship and warship. On Greek pottery there are many pictures of these handy merchant warships. They were used on voyages where there was a good chance of being attacked—which seems to have been most of the time, for the Greeks took to piracy in summer as naturally as modern people go to the seashore for a va-

Greek bireme, 500 B.C.

16 cation. Unlike the round cargo ships, these merchant warships employed a single row of oarsmen as well as a sail. Their long, sharp, narrow prow appears capable of carrying the ship through the water like a knife cutting through melon. It is possible that these were the "tramp" ships of their day, going from port to port without any set route or schedule.

The Greeks worked continually to improve their warships, for the city-states that made up Greece were always in conflict. When the city of Athens was at its height, the military leaders of Sparta and the merchants of Corinth grew jealous of her. War came. Squadrons of Greek warships fought each other, and Athens was defeated. The Greek historian Thucydides led one of these squadrons for his city, Athens. As a consequence of losing this battle he was exiled for twenty years, during which time he wrote a history of the war. In it he revealed a good deal about Greek "long" ships, as warships were then called.

Thucydides's summary of the long ship's history explains that at first Greek warships were *biremes*—ships similar to the Phoenicians', with two levels of oarsmen on each side. Then about 800 B.C. these biremes were fitted with powerful pointed rams. In battle, instead of boarding an enemy ship, the Greek warship's crew tried to slam into the other ship and sink her. Later a platform was added which ran down the center of the ship. This was the storming bridge. Men with spears and bows fought on this platform and often were the deciding factor in victory or defeat. These long ships fought near land. They did have a sail, but when the battle was about to begin the sail was left on shore and the ship "cleared for action." The oars, not the sail, were the "wings of the ship." When Thucydides himself commanded his squadron in 424 B.C., his ships were *triremes*—built with three rows of oarsmen to a side; 170 men worked the oars. These ships were about 150 feet long and extremely narrow.

Ships with still more oarsmen were built at various times by the Greeks. When Alexander the Great went out to conquer the East he built a fleet of ships with seven

Greek trireme, fifth century B.C.

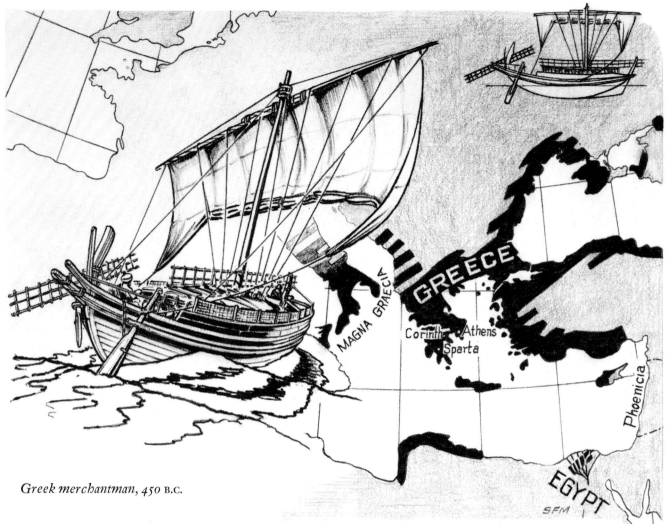

Greek merchantman, 450 B.C.

banks of oars. And by the time the Romans had begun their conquest of Greece, ships with sixteen banks of oars were being built. The Greeks undoubtedly recorded how the oars were arranged on these giants, but no descriptions have so far been discovered. This is one of the many unsolved puzzles about ancient ships.

The Greeks fought sea battles often, yet they had no full-time navy. Warships were generally built only in times of emergency and even then were used only during the warmer months. During the winter when the sea was rough and stormy, they stayed in their harbors. The ideal Greek port actually had two harbors, an outer harbor for commercial ships and a fortified inner harbor to protect the city from attack. An enemy ship trying to get into the inner harbor had to pass through a connecting channel, and if the ship succeeded in passing this defended channel it still had to face the triremes in the naval harbor. The men who worked these ships during battle were free citizens, not slaves, so they reported for duty and fought when it suited them. They also went home when they pleased, sometimes abandoning their ships before battle when they had work to do back on their farms. The loyalty of such crews could not be relied on, either;

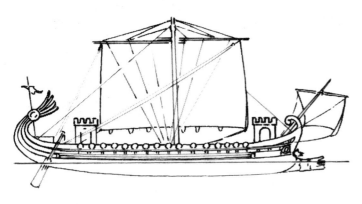

Roman trireme, about 30 B.C.

they often deserted to the enemy by the shipload when offered money, or when they believed that their side was certain of defeat. Probably many of those who fought at sea did so because they were too poor to equip themselves with the proper helmet and shield to join the army.

Although they have often been called great lovers of the sea, the Greeks seldom "went to sea" as we use the expression. By staying close to the coast, their ships traveled the length of the Mediterranean using headlands and islands as guides. A coastal guide called a *Stadiasmus* gave anchorage information and the distance between ports. At night the Greeks usually pulled their ships up to the beach and moored them with the stern facing toward land. In those dangerous times a wise captain kept the prow of his ship facing the open sea so that when he was attacked by land he could make a quick getaway. At night the crew cooked and slept on the beach, and at dawn they shoved off for another day's sailing or rowing.

The Romans, who replaced the Greeks as the dominant sea power of the Mediterranean world, were a nation of landlubbers. They did not take to the water until Rome went to war with Carthage, a Phoenician settlement in North Africa which, by virtue of her knowledge of trade routes, shipbuilding and navigation, was able to control the western Mediterranean, including the island of Sicily off the "toe" of Italy. Rome wanted Sicily, so for the first time in Roman history her army crossed the sea to drive out Carthage. But to conquer the Carthaginians Rome had to build fleet after fleet of warships. Within five years she had a navy of 120 fighting ships. Still, year after year the Romans lost their ships in storms and in defeat, and the war known in history as one of the Punic Wars went on for nearly twenty-four years. Finally, in 241 B.C., a Roman fleet of 200 warships defeated the Carthaginian fleet, and for the next 500 years Rome, a sea power at last, ruled the Mediterranean.

Rome claimed—and weary admirals in Carthage agreed—that she had won the war at sea partly because of a new boarding device on Roman ships. This was a grappler the Romans had invented called a *corvus,* or "crow." It was a gangplank made of heavy timbers that stood upright on the Roman ship. When the enemy came in close enough the timbers were dropped. Then an iron hook attached to the end of the crow held the enemy ship until the Romans could force their way aboard. The Romans were expert man-to-man fighters, and when they boarded a ship this aspect of their fighting power counterbalanced their deficiencies in seamanship.

The Romans built ships with many banks of oars, but they soon realized that the trireme was the best fighting ship. Their trireme was similar to the Greeks', but heavier and wider, with a smaller ram. A large square sail was carried on the mainmast and a small one, called an *artemon,* in front of the bow. In the stern, or sometimes amidship, a tower was built from which the Romans could fight.

The Liburnia, a pirate tribe on the Yugoslavian coast, developed a fighting ship that was adopted and improved on by the Romans: the Liburnian. Ships of this type can be seen in a relief carved shortly after 31 B.C. when the battle took place in which Antony and Cleopatra, soundly beaten by the adopted son of Julius Caesar, fled back to

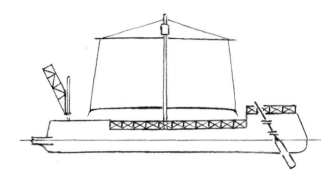

Quinquireme rigged with corvus. Roman, Punic Wars.

Egypt. It appears to be a bireme, but the carving does not show the details of the ship with much clarity, for what looks like a decorative trim along the side of the ship may actually be a row of shipped oars. The Liburnian helped the Romans to clear the Mediterranean Sea of pirates; now that the wealth of the provinces, especially the grain, could be carried safely to Rome, the sea was soon crowded with Roman ships.

The Romans never really took to the sea except as passengers: their fighting galleys were manned by slaves, and their merchant ships were mostly crewed by Phoenicians and other seafaring people. Yet Rome had the greatest merchant fleet in the ancient world. Gigantic Roman grain ships traded between Rome and Alexandria, a voyage of 1,200 miles, which generally was recorded as having taken from fifteen to twenty days but might actually have taken very much longer. Some of these grain ships were so large that it has been said that one such ship could supply the city of Athens with enough grain for a year. In addition to its cargo, such a ship also carried hundreds of passengers.

Roman merchant ships were so broad they looked almost round. They were from 90 to 150 feet long, and some were 45 feet wide and 45 feet deep, which made for plenty of cargo space. Cabins used by officers and traveling VIP's were situated at the stern. Rising from the stern of some cargo ships was a tall carved goose neck and head; on other cargo ships the curved stern terminated in an ornamental prong sweeping backward toward midship and flaring upward. Pictures of some of the Roman cargo ships show another mast that also carried a large sail and two triangular topsails. Perhaps these double-masted ships were as common in Roman times as the single-masted ships. With their curious ramlike bows they were similar to much earlier ships; in fact they look very much like the double-masted Cretan ships of centuries before.

Present-day underwater exploration techniques are helping to reveal a good deal about shipbuilding in ancient times. For instance, in 1967 divers examining ancient shipwrecks in the Mediterranean discovered some interesting things about Roman cargo ships. The planks were built carvel fashion: that is, edge to edge, as in Egyptian ships. They were so well matched that the swelling of the wood in water was enough to make the ship watertight. These thick planks were joined with pegs in the middle of the plank, the way a cabinet is put together. This made the hull of ancient cargo ships much stronger than had been suspected. In addition, the hull was covered with cloth soaked in tar, then covered with a thin layer of lead. Such advances in the art of shipbuilding in that period had not even been guessed at before, and there is reason to believe that many more surprises are in store as divers continue to make discoveries.

We do know that the Roman sea captains used a guide called a *Periplus*. This was a list of directions which might read: "Sailing from Ostia along the coast you will reach Ischia on your right and the bay on your left in two days. Good drinking water here. Dead ahead you will see a small island and a cape. . . ." The directions guided the captain down the coast of Italy, across to Sicily at Messina, then perhaps around to Marsala. A short sail from Marsala, it was possible to see the coast of North Africa.

Merchants on a grand scale, the Romans traded with China and had a fleet of more

than 100 ships that traveled regularly between the Red Sea and India. At her height
Rome had complete control of the eastern
and western Mediterranean as well as the
Black Sea. As a result of numerous invasions
by sea she conquered Britain. But during
the fifth century the Roman empire began
gradually to lose control of Europe to the
invading Germanic tribes. It was about this
time that the present-day nations began
slowly to take shape. To control the oceans
as well as the seas, and to develop worldwide trade monopolies, the emerging countries of western Europe began building ships
—sturdier vessels than those that had plied
the Nile, but with many features common
to those earlier ships.

After the decline of Rome the history of
ships sailing the Mediterranean is a blank
except for an occasional reference in ancient
manuscripts. But for hundreds of years shipbuilding continued to progress, for when we
see Mediterranean ships again in the ninth
century we find them so different as to
be startling. Mediterranean ships are now
carrying a triangular sail; the square sail is
gone. How the use of the three-cornered sail
came about, or why the square sail disappeared so completely, is a mystery. But two
things are certain: at this time the use of
triangular sails was a new feature on Mediterranean ships, and its use on these ships
was total. The "whys" and "wherefores" of
this historical fact remain hidden.

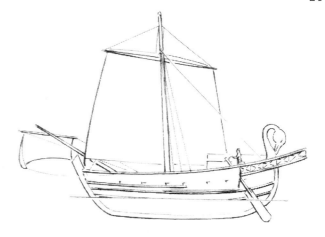

Roman merchantman, about A.D. *30.*

The Nydam boat, 75 ft. x 10 ft. 8 in. Excavated from Nydam peat bog near Schleswig, Denmark, 1863. Dated to about A.D. 300.

2

The Viking Adventure

CURIOUS puzzles in the history of shipbuilding are not restricted to the Mediterranean. Since the Romans saw ships with sails in France and Britain as early as 56 B.C., it is surprising that such great shipbuilders and explorers as the Scandinavians did not have ships with sails until more than five hundred years later. Not one of the ancient Scandinavian ships that have been found has any sign of a mast; and none of the thousands of rock engravings of Scandinavian ships drawn before A.D. 500 shows a ship with a sail.

The pieces of the history of Scandinavian ships click into place one by one. The story begins with a boat called the *Nydam boat,* which was built about A.D. 300. This was a coastal boat used by the early Scandinavians who lived in the northern countries where the mountains meet the sea. The Nydam boat appears to have been an excellent vessel for use on the enclosed Baltic Sea and along the coast of the North Sea. It was built of oak, and twenty-eight men pulled at its oars. There was no sail on this 75-foot-long craft. Both ends—for all early Scandinavian

ships were double-ended—curved slightly upward. There was a broad, thick plank at the bottom to which the other planks were attached to form a V-shaped hull. But the planks were fitted together differently from the carvel-built boats of the Mediterranean. The Nydam boat was clinker-built; that is, the planks overlapped like the boards of a clapboard house instead of being placed edge to edge. Each set of overlapped planks was riveted together with iron nails and washers.

The Nydam boat and others similar to it served the Scandinavians very well for a few hundred years. But about the seventh century two situations developed to create a demand for a new type of ship: there was a shortage of farmland, and trade with the south was expanding around such centers as Stockholm. Two ships found at Kralsund, in Norway, show how the challenge was met. The V-shaped hull is gone; instead, the ship is U-shaped in the middle to make it sturdier in the water. The stem and stern are high and sharply curved up into fine points. The method of building these ships was very much like that of building the later Viking

24 ships. And although no mast or sail has been found, these Kralsund boats could have carried both.

During the 700s the population of Scandinavia grew so rapidly that the land could no longer support the people, and the Norsemen added sails to their ships and took to the sea. At first many of them sailed off on raiding parties. In the mid-800s a huge fleet of 600 Viking ships sailed up the Elbe and destroyed Hamburg. A Viking leader named Ragnar Lodbrok led another 120 ships up the Seine and took Paris. These Scandinavians were not merely pirates. They were interested in trade and in acquiring land for settlement. They built the town in Ireland that later became Dublin. They settled in England and became excellent farmers and traders. In Russia they traded fox and beaver throughout the land, and built trading

centers that became great cities; they even went on to become the ruling Grand Dukes. They were given land in the part of France that became Normandy, the strongest and best organized section of that country. The Scandinavians were excellent administrators and vigorously enforced law and order wherever they settled. To almost all parts of Europe and a portion of Asia these people from the north brought a new vitality and progress that had been missing since the fall of Rome. In this way, Viking ships put European history on a different track, as ships were often to do in the centuries following.

In 1962 a Viking long ship, or sailing warship, was discovered in the harbor of the Danish city of Roskilde. It is 100 feet long, with a keel well worn from having been dragged ashore many times. It held fifty or

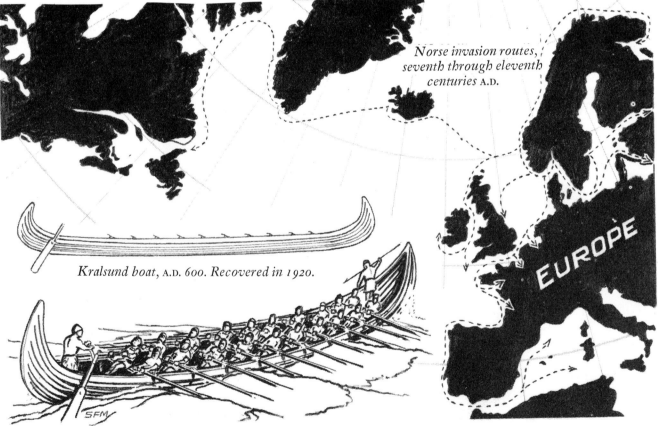

Norse invasion routes, seventh through eleventh centuries A.D.

Kralsund boat, A.D. *600. Recovered in 1920.*

EUROPE

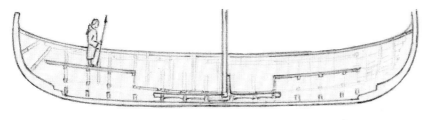

Profile of the wrecked knarr, 54 ft. x 14 ft. 9 in., recovered at Roskilde Fjord in 1968. Dated to A.D. 1000.

sixty fighting men and was light enough to be rowed at a good clip. It was clinker-built, and as in all Viking ships the planks had been shaped with axes. Four other early Viking ships were found sunk along with this warship, one a cargo ship called a *knarr*. Until this discovery no one was absolutely certain what a *knarr* looked like.

The *knarr* was used by the Scandinavians on their trips to Iceland where they established settlements. Actually, Iceland was probably first visited by the Irish in large hide boats called *curachs* years before the Scandinavians took to the open sea. But the only Irish to use the island were a few hermit monks, while the Scandinavians settled in and began farming and fishing. On one of these voyages to Iceland in a *knarr*, a Scandinavian sailor named Gunnbjorn was blown off course and discovered Greenland. He did not, however, go ashore, and some time later

Eric the Red determined to rediscover the land Gunnbjorn had described. He sailed from Iceland into the prevailing easterly winds of early summer and after forty-four days landed in Greenland. Three years later with twenty-five ships he made a return trip to build a settlement. Only fourteen of the ships arrived. Some of them sank and others were forced to turn back, which gives some idea of how tough the passage was.

According to the facts disclosed by the investigators of the Roskilde find, the *knarr* in which Eric the Red sailed probably was a tubby-looking oceangoing ship. Clinker-built, doubled-ended, it had only one rudder, on the right side. The rudder side was called the "steer-board" side, from which came "starboard," the right side of a ship. (The other side was called "port" because it was the side turned toward the dock. The side rudder might be damaged if the star-

board side were shoved against the dock in port.)

These wide, spacious cargo ships also carried Scandinavians to Vineland, an old name for North America, some 500 years before Columbus landed on an island in the Caribbean. How this came about is an amusing story. A young Icelander, Bjarni Herjolfson, went to spend the winter in Norway. While he was away his father sold his land and sailed off with Eric the Red to settle in Greenland. When Bjarni Herjolfson returned to Iceland he set sail to follow his father. A fog came up, and the wind blew his ship past Greenland. He sailed on to discover North America. Unimpressed with what he saw, he turned his ship around and this time reached Greenland. Everyone, even his father, ridiculed Bjarni for not going ashore and exploring the new land.

Eric the Red's son Leif heard Bjarni's story. He bought Bjarni's ship and, following Bjarni Herjolfson's course, landed at Newfoundland with a crew of thirty-five. A member of that crew named Tyrkir found vines and grapes. That is how the name Vineland, or Wineland, came about. Leif Ericson's words come to us through the centuries and indicate the businesslike attitude Norsemen took when it came to shipping. On this great day when the Norseman first set foot on the North American continent, he had this to say to his crew: "Now, we have two jobs. On alternate days we have to gather grapes and cut vines and fell timber, so as to provide a cargo of such things for my ship." Greenlanders attempting to settle in North America a few years later stayed on for only two years before the hostility of the natives forced them to leave. During their stay Thorfinn Karlsenfni's wife gave birth to a son, Snorri, the first child of European parentage born in America—approximately a thousand years ago.

There is a good deal more to add to the story of the Scandinavians and of their incredible ships, whose flexibility, called "give," made them such wonderful oceangoing vessels. For example, the men rowed with a short sweep of the oars, which was much more effective than the long-drawn-out sweep. It is interesting, also, that they did not sit on the thwarts when they rowed; in fact, there were no thwarts, or cross-beams, above deck. What the Viking oarsmen used for seats can only be guessed at: possibly the chests or footlockers that held their gear.

Two famous and beautiful ships from the Viking period are on display in a museum in Oslo. One, called the Oseberg ship, was built about A.D. 840, the other, the Gokstad ship, about 900. The Oseberg and Gokstad ships were found in Norwegian burial mounds—large hills of soil, stone and clay in which the ships were buried along with their owners. The Oseberg ship could have been used as a coastal ship, while the Gokstad ship is larger and sturdier and could easily have been an oceangoing vessel. The latter could sail, as was proved when a replica made a voyage across the Atlantic in 1893 to take part in the Chicago World's Fair. Commanded by Captain Magnus Andersen, the ship left Bergen, Norway, on April 30. At three o'clock on the morning of May 27 the east coast of Newfoundland was sighted. The ship had sailed through high seas and storms. In one severe gale it lay to (stopped with prow headed into the wind) for eight hours with a drag or sea anchor out. Hardly any two stories written about the replica

The Oseberg ship when unearthed in 1904.
Drawn from a photograph.

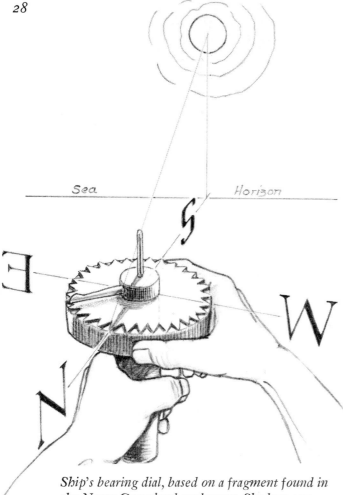

Ship's bearing dial, based on a fragment found in the Norse Greenland settlement. Shadow cast by the sun at midday pointed true north. Other directions were thereby established on the 32-point dial scale. Pointer rotated when the handle was oriented to the ship's heading.

agree on its size. The *Scientific American* in June 1893 gave the length as 78 feet. In August the same journal wrote that the length was "only 74 feet." Other reports claim the ship was either 72 or 76 feet long. This variance in measurement is common even with contemporary writers. Sometimes the length of the keel is given; again the extreme length from stem to stern is quoted, and at still other times the length *between* the sternpost and the stempost is reported. To further complicate matters, sometimes the length of the hull at water level is taken as the ship's length.

Although some people still believe that the Norsemen used only the flight of birds, the formation and movement of clouds, the color of the ocean itself, and the movement of the ocean currents as guides to find their position at sea, they actually had much more workmanlike and complicated guides: the sun-stone and sun charts. The sun charts gave the position of the sun at dawn and at noon in a particular latitude every day of the year. The Norsemen would sail north or south along the coast until they were in the same latitude as their destination across the ocean. Then they would keep to this particular latitude. The sun-stone was used to find the sun when it was obscured by fog or clouds.

The end of the Viking age came swiftly. Ireland erupted in bloody war, and the Vikings were defeated and forced to leave. Among themselves the Scandinavian states fought fearful battles continually, and this sapped their strength. Iceland declared its independence and set up a separate legislative body, the Althing. In England the Danes lost out to the Anglo-Saxons in the battle for control. In Russia the Swedish nobility began a gradual merging with the local families. The fingers of the hand that had gripped Europe so firmly for years were being chopped off one at a time. What remained by the middle of the eleventh century was not just a memory, but a force; and part of that force was felt in the sturdy ships, patterned after the Vikings', that were being built in France and England and other western European countries—ships that helped to shape the future for all the world.

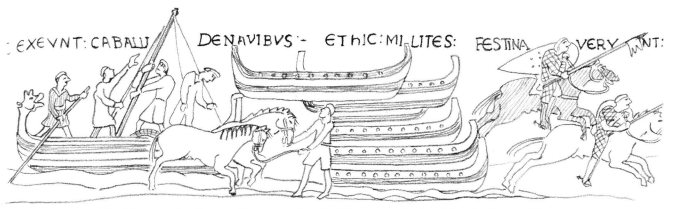

: EXEVNT: CABALLI DE NAVIBVS · ET hIC MI LITES: FESTINA VERVNT :

The Norman landing on Pevensey Beach, Wessex, as depicted by the Bayeux Tapestry.

*Warships of
William the Conqueror,
Pevensey Beach,
September 28, 1066.*

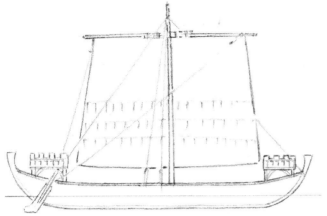

Thirteenth-century English warship.
Crusaders debarking at Venice.

3.
North and South:
The Clash of Traditions

WILLIAM, Duke of Normandy, a descendant of the Vikings, invaded England and conquered her in 1066. The ships he used were changed very little from earlier Viking craft. It was not until thirty years later, with the beginning of the Crusades, that European ships began to develop along new lines. Ships from the north sailed down into the Mediterranean, and Italian ships from the great commercial city-states of Venice, Pisa, and Genoa carried hundreds of thousands of Christian European crusaders and their supplies to the Mohammedan Near East. For 200 years the Christians tried to hold Jerusalem. In the end, after great loss of life, the relatively backward Europeans were defeated by the culturally superior Mohammedans. During this long war the shipowners of north and south learned from each other important things about ships and shipping that were later to help them dominate the oceans of the world.

One of the ideas the north borrowed from the south was the use of the compass at sea. The magnetic compass probably came to the Mediterranean from the Orient. At first it was a crude instrument such as you yourself can make utilizing a bowl of water, a needle stuck at a right angle through a wooden match, and a magnet. Here is how: Float the needle on the water. Move the magnet clockwise around the outside of the bowl a few times. Then, suddenly remove the magnet. You will find that the needle will point north and south. (Don't use a metal pot or bowl: the needle will up-end and cling to the side.) A crude compass made in this fashion was used by seamen only in fog or during cloudy weather. The Italian mariners improved on it, putting it into a box and balancing the needle on a fine point. Perfected in this way it was built into ships and used for navigation in all weathers.

During the Crusades northern seamen became familiar with and began to use to a limited degree the triangular sail of the southern, or Latin, countries. The "Latin" sail, later called *lateen,* ran in the same direction as the boat's keel—fore-and-aft. The northern square sail was hung running from one side of the ship to the other.

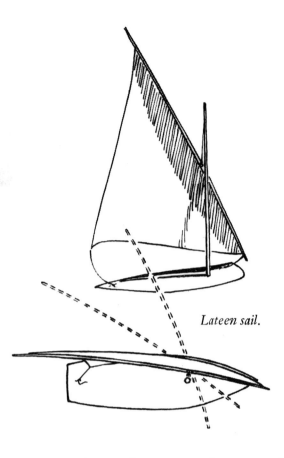

Lateen sail.

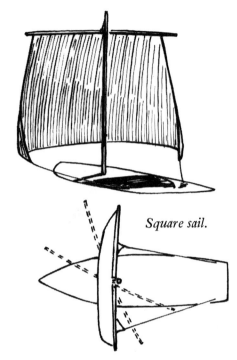

Square sail.

In the Mediterranean, shipowners began to adopt the long stern rudder being used in the north. Stern rudders were not a new feature on ships. Boat models with large rudders tied directly over the stern have been found in the tomb of Meket-Rē, a wealthy Theban official in the time of Pharaoh Mentu-hotep, who ruled Egypt two thousand years before Christ. They were also used in the Orient and can be seen in temple carvings in India from as early as A.D. 800. In Europe the stern rudder seems to have been first used in the north in the late 1100s. However, some researchers think it was used in Genoa before that time in stout oarlike form, but that it did not really catch on until the rudder was hinged onto the strong sternposts of northern ships. Where it originally came into use in European waters is not so important as the fact that it gradually took

hold and was improved on in the heavy seas of the north.

The benefits of the stern rudder can best be understood by visualizing how a ship with the steering oar at the side would behave in high wind or rough weather. Over the ship goes, leaning so hard that the steering oar is lifted out of the water, allowing the wind to blow the ship this way or that, possibly moving it far off course. With a heavy keel and with the stern rudder strongly hinged to a solid sternpost, the ship's hull offers more resistance to the wind and the impact of the water and helps to stabilize the vessel. Another advantage of the stern rudder in either storm or calm is that the water coming toward it along the sides of the ship's hull gives the ship more maneuverability as well as a firmer "grip" in the water.

There were other advantages to using a

stern rudder, and it would be reasonable to assume that shipowners in the early 1200s would have instructed their shipwrights to build the new feature immediately into all ships. But the switchover from side-oar rudder to stern rudder took place gradually over many years, as changes in ship handling, building and rigging usually do. Ships are expensive craft. Trade vessels were then and still are often kept in service as long as a hundred years. Even today, ships built more than a century ago still sail from U.S. ports to England, the Middle East and the Orient carrying barley, wheat, corn or soybeans, and they still turn a profit. All through history, older ships have continued to sail with newer and more efficient ships.

Commercial or national rivalries often help speed the adoption of improved methods of shipbuilding and navigation. For instance, in the Mediterranean the compass was adopted so quickly because it enabled a merchant vessel to make two voyages a year instead of one. Also, a ship no longer needed to sail from headland to headland, but could use more direct routes on the open sea. To use a compass paid in hard cash. Shipowners build and use ships to make money, and improvements that do not increase profits are not accepted so readily as those that do. A ship is not obsolete so long as it is satisfactory for the work required of it, regardless of how much a newer type of vessel might improve living conditions for the seamen. In commercial shipping this is as true in our own Nuclear Age as it was during the Middle Ages (1100–1400). However, the record of governments adopting new and improved designs for naval vessels is a fairly good one, for national survival has often de-

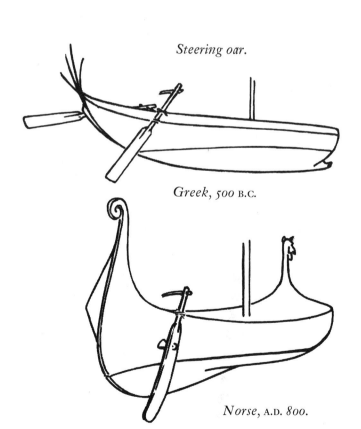

Steering oar.

Greek, 500 B.C.

Norse, A.D. *800.*

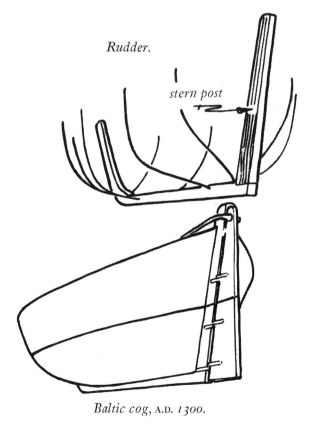

Rudder.

stern post

Baltic cog, A.D. *1300.*

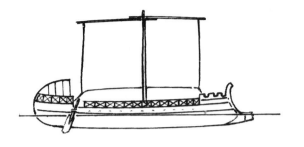

*Roman war galley,
second century* A.D., *40 oars.*

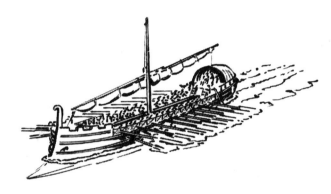

Byzantine dromen, 200 rowers.
A.D. *950.*

pended on the quality of a country's fighting ships.

The history of the adoption of the *bowsprit* is an example of the slowness involved in changes aboard ships. During the late Middle Ages the bowsprit was a common feature on most ships. "Sprit" was an early Saxon word that meant "to sprout," and the bowsprit was the spar or pole that "sprouted" from the bow. The bowsprit was used to carry the ropes, or, as they are called aboard ship, the lines, that were attached to the square sail. These lines, controlled by pulleys, kept the sail from flapping. (A sail that does not flap makes better use of the wind.)

Short projections at the bow can be seen on models of very early Egyptian ships. Roman ships had a spar jutting out from the bow; it carried a small square foresail. After this its popularity varied from time to time. It finally came into general use during this period on ships carrying a square sail, and it remained in use until the close of the age of large sailing vessels. Bowsprits are not needed on ships rigged only with the triangular lateen sail, unless as decoration or to carry a square foresail before the bow, because the lateen is a very versatile sail and can be shifted from fore-and-aft position to run from side to side and can therefore take advantage of almost all winds.

During the Middle Ages the kings and rulers of Europe waged war at sea using merchant ships as their fighting vessels. These merchant warship fleets were called the "Army by Sea" in documents of the time, and mostly that is exactly what they were: they transported the nobles, the soldiers, their horses and supplies across the sea to fight on the enemy's land. When a sea battle did take place, the objective was either to ram into and sink the enemy ship, or to board and fight hand to hand. Forts, or castles, were built onto the prow and stern in preparation for war. Soldiers defended these castles just as they defended castles on land. At the end of the war the castles were removed and the ships returned to commercial use.

This method of fighting changed somewhat with the introduction of guns, which were first carried aboard ship in the 1300s. The first small cannon were used in an attempt to shoot the sailors or troops aboard an enemy ship as they worked or fought: these guns could not greatly damage the ship itself. Cannon that could inflict serious damage to a ship were developed much later.

In the south, galleys—slender, oar-propelled warships—were used to fight other galleys. Incidentally, it was during one such battle between the galleys of Venice and Genoa that Marco Polo was taken prisoner. With plenty of time on his hands in a Genoese jail he wrote the story of his adventures at the court of Kublai Khan in China.

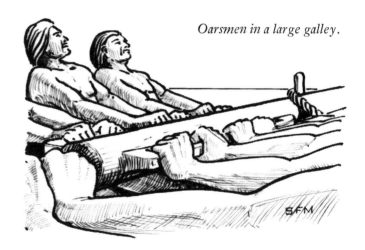

Oarsmen in a large galley.

Venice was the leader in commerce and shipbuilding in southern Europe, with Genoa a close second. These two port cities which controlled much of the land surrounding them were forced into trade on a large scale at first because, with the rapid increase in population during the early Middle Ages, they could not feed themselves. They found it necessary to import their bulky foodstuffs on slow, round merchant ships from areas where grain and fish were plentiful and food prices were low. These ships often went in convoy. Convoys sometimes had galleys as escorts, but more often they depended on their size for defense. Round cargo ships could be rammed by enemy galleys, but their sides were so high that it was difficult for the fighting men from the galleys to get aboard. These hulking cargo ships in the south were often built to carry two lateen sails on separate masts, and by the 1300s they had a solid castlelike structure aft, which helped in the ship's defense. And since southern trade was branching out into the Atlantic, stern rudders were introduced because they were practical on such voyages. Southern ships also began to carry square sail, a return to an old tradition.

Italian cities, however, profited mainly from the luxury trade they carried on with the East. Italian ships took eastern luxury goods to northern Europe; jewels, spices, silks and dyes made up the cargoes aboard merchant galleys. The most important item they carried on their return trips back to Italy from the north was gold, which for a while made Italian cities the banking centers of Europe. In fact, gold grew so scarce in the north that the only coins minted for a time were silver pennies.

Their relative immunity from piracy and their speed made the long, slim galleys excellent transports for high-priced low-bulk goods. These narrow war or cargo galleys were very much like the earlier Mediterranean biremes and triremes. The larger ships were manned by from 50 to almost 100 oarsmen to a side in two or three banks. The smaller galleys had a single row of oars to a side, each with perhaps 12, 19, or 28 oarsmen, or whatever number the shipwright decided best suited the particular task the galley was built to perform. At this early date the oarsmen were free sailors, not slaves, and they worked in times of danger, or getting in and out of port. At sea the gal-

leys were propelled by a large lateen sail hanging from a yard that was sometimes longer than the ship itself. But waiting for a favorable wind to carry a ship into a harbor sometimes took days or weeks, and at such times the oarsmen could row directly into the harbor and gain an advantage in time over ships that had to wait for the wind to take them to the docks.

Since the power of Venice and the livelihood of her citizens depended on trade, the Venetians were diligent sailors and shipbuilders. The city built an arsenal where fleets of galleys for war and trade were built. Three nobles were appointed Lords of the Arsenal. They were responsible for supervising the work and reporting on the fleet's condition. It was not enough merely to glance around and declare that everything was shipshape: the nobles were instructed to "see and feel" all the rigging and arms. The Venetians in fact developed such a cult of the sea that each year the Doge, or Duke of Venice, ceremoniously married the sea. He boarded a galleylike gilded barge called the *Bucentauro*, which carried "crimson and cloth-of-gold canopies," and tossed a wedding ring into the water, saying: "I marry you, O sea, in sign of your perpetual domination."

Because of their crafty and assiduous bargaining, the Venetians were disliked by most of their European customers. But since they had a virtual monopoly on all the precious items that were becoming so popular, it was either deal with them or do without. The spices for which many people had acquired a taste during the Crusades so improved the palatability of unrefrigerated food that they seemed a necessity. Taxes and rents in Europe were often assessed and paid in pep-

Twelfth-century war galley, Mediterranean.

Lateen-rigged Venetian merchantman of about 1300.

38   per; a pound of ginger was worth the price of a sheep, and a pound of mace would buy three sheep or half a cow. It is not surprising that Venice grew rich, or that later in history wars were fought for the control of the spice trade.

In addition to the output of the State Arsenal, private shipbuilders built galleys to be used in commerce or added to the city's fleet during war. They also began to build a ship called a *nef* (from the French word meaning ship, which in turn was derived from the Latin *nave*) patterned after one that had originated in the north, where it was called a *cog*. Cogs sailed without oars, and in battle these single-masted ships with square sail could not be so easily handled as the galleys. But, being roomier because they were broadly built, they were used to carry troops and supplies.

The cog was also used by the Venetians to curb piracy, because the pirates used a similar sailing ship. In fact cogs were introduced into southern waters by pirates based in France. Merchants attacked by such pirate ships saw the advantages of cogs and soon began to build them. These ships had strong stern rudders. They were long-keeled and at first were built with straight endposts; later the sternpost developed an upward curve and grew rounded. The single square sail on a cog was fitted with *reefpoints*, short pieces of rope inserted in lines across the sail and used to tie it into a roll when it was shortened. *Bonnets* were also used at this time: strips of canvas laced to the foot of the sail. When the wind was slight the bonnets were added; when it was strong they were removed. Cogs were clinker-built even in southern waters, which

Baltic cog of about 1350.

Mediterranean cog of 1450.

indicates their northern origin. Solid-looking castles soon appeared as part of the stern. Forecastles became smaller as time passed, and eventually they too were built into the prow. Finally, when the castles on the cog became part of the ship itself, the difference between warships and trade ships in the north disappeared.

To the traders in the Middle Ages and afterward, it must have seemed sometimes that there were more pirates at sea than honest merchants. Cogs and other ships still had to stay close to the coast. If they were driven ashore during a storm, or because of damage or accident, the cargo could be held by the lord of the land where the ship went aground. The lord could also hold passengers and crew for ransom. Under certain circumstances he could even sell his prisoners as servants or workers for a period of time, or, as was more common in earlier

days, as slaves. So voyages were risky undertakings. Travelers confessed their sins before boarding ship and gave thanks at the nearest shrine when they landed safely.

The cog is one of the many "little ships" that were more important to ship development than many of the so-called great ships. Cogs worked in war and peace. They were well suited for long-distance trade along the coasts of northern and southern Europe. They carried food long distances. More food meant that more people were able to live in towns and cities. Since they did not have to raise crops, the city people had the time and the manpower to develop industries such as the manufacture of woolen textiles. Cloth made in the city could be traded for Baltic grain or Icelandic fish. Now ordinary people, not just lords and ladies, were able to be really free men and not semifree serfs chained to the land. In this way the cog

40 helped people to live a freer and more civilized life.

To the north the cog brought commercial power. During the thirteenth century a group of German trading cities banded together to form the Hanseatic League. The League built up a navy to guard its commerce from pirates and even fought and won wars against Denmark. It controlled trade on the Baltic and North seas. It had a monopoly on the Baltic herring fisheries. Fish, lumber, grain, and a few manufactured goods, under the protection of Hanseatic naval power, could be shipped cheaply for long distances.

The Hanseatic League established trading stations in leading trade centers such as London and Bruges. The Hanseatic cog carried the wool of England to other parts of Europe, giving England a good trade base on which to grow. League ships traded with

Limits of the Hanseatic League, fourteenth, fifteenth centuries. Seventy or more towns traded within the Hanse.

Bergen
Novgorod
London
Lübeck
Bruges
Crakow
Rouen

Bruges in Flanders, which at that time was larger than London and was the distribution center of the north. Almost any item from any part of the world could be bought or sold in Bruges. But the city had a difficult time keeping her channel to the sea open, for it often silted up, and when heavier ships than the cog came into general use the city ceased to exist as a great seaport and trading center.

The Hanseatic cog was a vessel suited to its time. It was especially important since the good roads built by the Romans in the north had been allowed to deteriorate during the early Middle Ages. Since land travel was slow and dangerous, the rivers of Europe had come into use more and more for transporting goods. But the nobles had seen a chance to grow rich by charging tolls to those who traveled on their rivers. Merchants employing barges and river craft had to pay heavily at the nobles' toll stations. So they began to use the seagoing cog to avoid the rivers. New ports were built all over Europe to handle this seagoing trade. Old ports such as London began to boom.

Commerce became the important means by which the governments of Europe could expand and carry on in both war and peace. Rulers offered encouragement to the merchants, giving them privileges and charters and getting money in return. Kings no longer had to depend solely on their nobles for the money and the men necessary to control their people and wage wars. With the backing of rich merchants and trading towns, a king had money to hire an army with which to support a strong central government. This commercial growth created a lively Europe, and nowhere was this liveliness felt with greater force than in shipbuilding.

Baltic cog, A.D. *1350.*

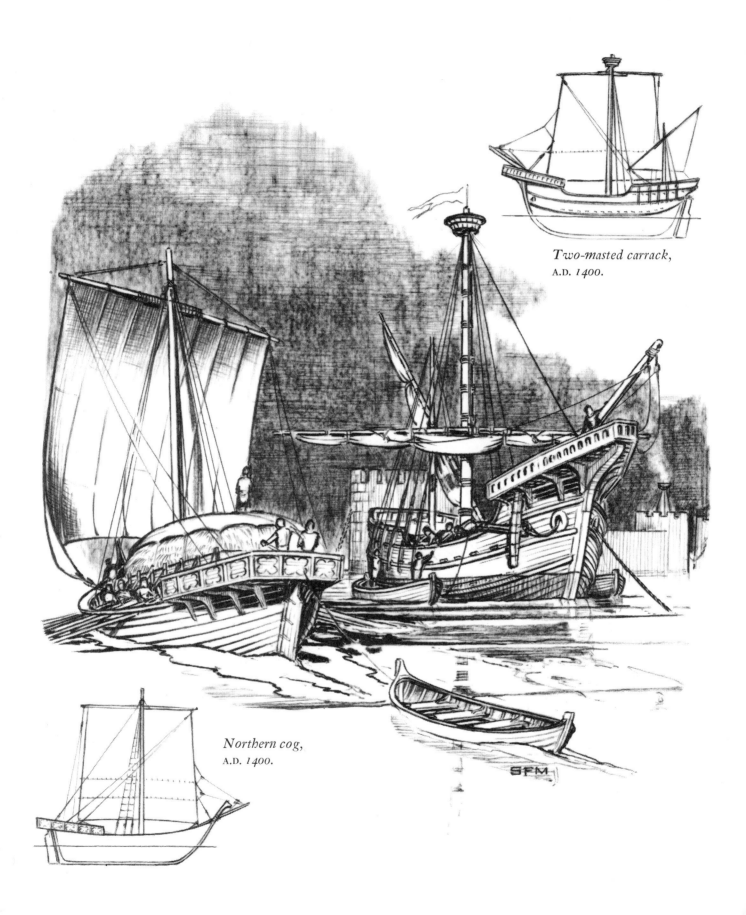

Two-masted carrack,
A.D. *1400.*

Northern cog,
A.D. 1400.

4.

The Leap in the Dark: 1492

IT WAS during the fifteenth century that European ships really began to sail the open oceans of the world. Until the time of the voyages of Columbus most men thought the Atlantic impossible to cross. Scientifically thinking men had known the world was a globe since the ancient Greeks proved it mathematically. But people in general believed, with the monk who wrote just a few years before Columbus sailed, that: "It is impossible to reach the other side of the globe because of the vast extent of the ocean, which it is impossible for any of our shipping to cross." Or, as a diplomat explained as he looked out at the Atlantic in 1465: "They say the water is so turbulent no one can cross it. It is said that some have tried, by sailing in galleys and ships, but not one of them has returned." But ships built during the 1400s could cross the Atlantic. There were men who would make the trip, and they would return.

In order to accomplish this feat, sailing ships underwent the greatest changes in their history during the 1400s. These changes had been gradually taking place along separate lines. The south was building the northern cogs, and the north tried—unsuccessfully—to adapt the galley to northern waters. During the Third Crusade in 1191 Richard the Lionhearted of England sailed in a one-masted ship into the Mediterranean. There he was forced to fight an Arab ship. He happened to win the battle, probably because as a king he carried so many fighting men on his ship. The Arab craft was a carvel-built three-masted ship with lateen sails. The young warrior king had sailed in a clinker-built single-masted ship with a square sail. During the previous centuries these two shipbuilding traditions had been clashing; now they merged. The result was a carvel-built three-masted ship with both square and lateen sails, a stern rudder, and high fore and aft castles built in as a permanent and useful part of the hull. This ship was called a *carrack,* and carracks eventually replaced the cog as the most important long-distance cargo carriers of Europe.

There is a wonderfully detailed drawing of a carrack done by a Flemish artist about 1470. The hull is carvel-built and strength-

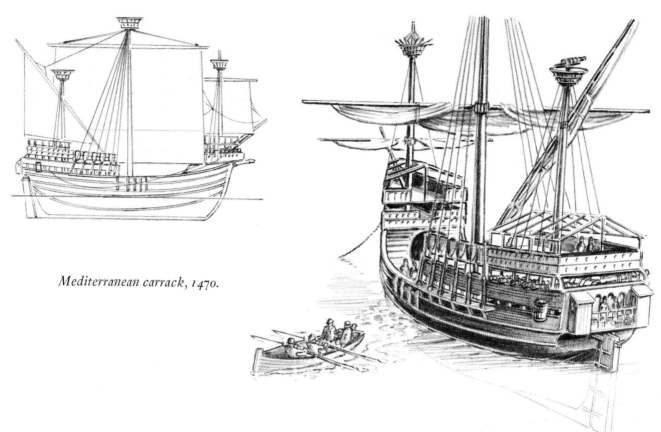

Mediterranean carrack, 1470.

ened by wales and skids. Wales are heavy timbers installed as a continuous band in the outside of the hull, above the water level, to help strengthen a ship. They run from stem to stern along the ship's side, and they are usually thicker and broader than the planking used in the ship's hull. Skids are vertical pieces of timber which form a sort of outside frame to reinforce the hull above the water.

The carrack's three masts, running from bow to stern, are called foremast, mainmast and mizzenmast. The sail on the mizzenmast is lateen; the other two masts carry square sails. All are topped by structures like crow's nests. Spears or lances that were used in battle can be seen in the fore and main topping structures in the Flemish drawing, and the mizzen top has what appears to be a small gun set up as if it were swiveled.

There are five cannon to a side placed on the aftercastle deck, now called the quarterdeck. Above the quarterdeck is the half-deck, and there are two decks to the forecastle. Compared to the simple single-masted cog, the carrack was a complex craft.

By 1500, as can be seen in paintings of European harbors made at that time, this type of ship often carried another mast, a *bonaventure mizzen,* with a lateen sail. The bonaventure, sometimes called the outer mizzen, was the fourth mast (behind the mizzenmast). Later it was used on other types of ships. Also common in pictures of ships during this century were *ratlines,* which had been in use in the north in the early 1200s but did not appear on the Mediterranean until much later. Ratlines are pieces of rope ranged in a ladderlike fashion along a set of shrouds; they form rope steps for going up and down the rigging. Since pirates were a constant danger, especially the Turkish pirates in the south, in these paintings we see that carracks were heavily armed, carrying as many as 56 small cannon; sometimes more. Merchant ships in all seas carried some iron cannon, and the men were armed with handguns.

Another kind of ship commonly used in the 1400s and later, often referred to as the Portuguese *caravel,* was probably in use much earlier as a fishing vessel. But it was in the 1400s that the caravel took to the ocean. On this ship the mainmast was amidship and the other two masts were behind it, toward the stern. At first it carried lateen sails on all three masts. However, when the caravel went to sea it was rerigged with a square mainsail and sometimes a square foresail. The *Pinta* and the *Nina,* the two

ships that accompanied Columbus's *Santa Maria* in 1492, were caravels. It was probably also in caravels that the Portuguese sailors sent out by Prince Henry the Navigator explored over 2,000 miles of African coastline. Prince Henry's seamen also went out into the open ocean to colonize Madeira, the Azores, the Cape Verde Islands, and the Canaries. All of these settlements became essential way stations in later voyages of discovery. These geographical explorations in the swift, low-hulled caravels proved that ships could sail a thousand miles into the Atlantic and return safely.

Prince Henry died in 1460. In 1488 Bartholomew Dias succeeded in rounding the Cape of Good Hope. Dias named it the Cape of Storms, but John II, who was king of Portgual, renamed it Good Hope in the belief that Dias's voyage promised that a

Mediterranean caravel, lateen-rigged, A.D. *1500.*

Caravel, square-rigged fore and main.

direct sea route to India could be found by going around Africa. Dias sailed four times the distance covered by Columbus, and he was on the open seas, out of sight of land, three times as long.

Portuguese ships and men did reach India later, under the leadership of Vasco da Gama, whose great voyage to the Orient began in 1497. Da Gama arrived at the Cape Verde Islands with three ships; then, instead of following the Atlantic coast, as was the general practice, he took the more direct course to the Cape of Good Hope out of sight of land, reaching the southern tip of Africa in ninety-three days. A story is told that his captains threatened to turn back on this leg of the voyage. Da Gama called them to his ship, and while they were there he had the navigating instruments aboard their ships thrown into the sea. Therefore, since they had no choice, they had to follow him. The story is probably not true. For one thing, during the 1400s any good captain would have kept most of his navigational knowledge in that human instrument, his brain. Tossing their astrolabes overboard might have inconvenienced da Gama's captains, but it would not have prevented them from leaving his convoy and heading home.

After rounding the Cape, da Gama's ship was blown into the Antarctic, a fearful sea. An iceberg was sighted. Under ordinary circumstances da Gama might have stopped and replenished his water supply, for sailing ships sometimes obtained drinking water from pools of melted ice on icebergs; however, the iceberg da Gama encountered seemed to follow the ship, and this frightened the superstitious crew. But they managed to outrun that danger, sailing north into Arab waters, where they hired an Arab to guide the ship across the Indian Ocean. Da Gama clashed many times with the Arab traders, who were angry because the Portuguese had broken their spice monopoly with Venice, and barely escaped from the Orient with his life. He lost two of his ships and most of his men and did not reach home until 1499.

His return marked the opening of one of the world's richest trade routes. The cargo da Gama carried back to Portugal was worth sixty times the cost of the expedition. Thereafter it was possible for Portugal to compete with Venice in the European market.

At the close of the 1400s Portugal, hemmed in on land by Spain and far overshadowed in commerce by the Italians and by the trading centers of the north, looked toward the sea as the only means of commercial and physical expansion. On da Gama's first trip to the Orient he took a fleet of four ships carrying only twenty small cannon. On his second voyage in 1502 he commanded a large fleet, many men, and enough artillery and gunpowder to let the East know Europe had arrived. His purpose was not only to trade but to conquer, and he won for the Portuguese crown Mozambique in Africa and Goa in India.

The success of da Gama's military expedition was due in part to the cannon on his ships. The Portuguese could handily defeat any Arab fleet sent against them. Even in India, where guns and gunpowder were familiar items, many an oriental ruler bowed in submission because of the aggressive use of cannon, the ferocity and cruelty of the European sailors, and the judicious use of sturdily constructed and intricately rigged ships.

Lisbon

Cape Verde
Isls.

Calicut

Vasco da Gama,
1460–1524.

Cape of Good Hope, voyage of 1497–98.

Portugal had been sending out ships of exploration for many years when an Italian seaman, Christopher Columbus, approached the king of Portugal with the idea of sailing westward across the Atlantic to reach the mainland of Asia. King John II, who later assumed the title of "Lord of the Conquest, Navigation, and Commerce of Ethiopia, Arabia, Persia, and China," turned Columbus down, saying he already knew there was a continent in that direction, but that he was not interested in further investigation. These words are recorded, but no one has proved conclusively that the Portuguese knew about the American continents. Perhaps it was just his polite way of discouraging someone he thought insane. But Columbus persisted. He went on to Spain, where after many years he received financial backing. The history of Spain and indeed the world was changed by the voyages of this determined navigator.

Columbus's fleet which crossed the Atlantic consisted of three ships and about ninety men. They sailed from Spain on August 3, 1492; arrived at the Canary Islands on August 11, remaining there until September 6; and then headed westward. On the evening of October 11 the sailors saw petrels flying and a green reed floating in the water. Then a sailor on the *Pinta* sighted land. The next day the ships reached a small island and Columbus landed. Technically—and there are many people who dote on this technicality —the West Indies had been discovered, not the American continent. However, it was Columbus's voyages that aroused European interest in America. It was because of them that the Americas came under the influence of Europe, culturally, politically and in matters of religion. In fact, Columbus's voyages

and the publicity they received motivated others to cross the Atlantic after him. So, in the true sense of the word discovery, that is, "making known," Columbus *did* discover America.

Much research has been done on the three ships that took part in Columbus's first voyage. His flagship, the *Santa Maria,* was wrecked in the West Indies before Columbus returned to Spain. Columbus called the *Santa Maria* a *nao.* It is generally agreed that it was a ship of the carrack type, or, as some authorities say, it "somewhat" resembled a carrack. It must be kept in mind that in the 1400s ships were not "scientifically" constructed: they followed the "rule of thumb" rather than blueprints. Each seaport had its own idea of how a certain type of ship should be built. It sometimes happened that one sank before it got out of the harbor. But when a ship proved seaworthy the design was copied, with whatever improvements the shipbuilders in that particular area thought workable. The carrack, the caravel, the cog—these are *kinds* of ships. To use a modern example: the earliest aircraft carriers had no flight deck, because seaplanes were used, and these were hoisted on and off deck with cranes. Then came the converted liners and merchant ships on which flight decks were built. Today, aircraft carriers are the largest ships in the navy. But as a class, type or kind, these examples are all referred to as aircraft carriers.

In a log he kept (a practice years ahead of his time), Columbus mentions the sails on the *Santa Maria.* He says: "I let them set all sails, the main course with two bonnets, the fore course, the spritsail, the mizzen, the topsail and the boat's sail on the half deck."

Christopher Columbus
1451–1506

after the portrait in the Civico
Museo Archeologico, Como, thought
by some scholars to be genuine.
There is no known authenticated
portrait of Columbus.

50 The spritsail before the bow was square, as were the main and fore sails. Columbus grumbled that the *Santa Maria* was "not fit for voyages of discovery." But he thought highly of the swifter *Nina*, a caravel like the *Pinta*.

On his second voyage to the West Indies in 1493 Columbus commanded seventeen ships and 1,500 men—sailors, churchmen, and colonists. With this expedition the colonization and further exploration of America began. It is a sad fact that the great voyages of discovery were followed by war and the conquest of the so-called discovered countries. In addition, European settlers brought with them diseases that killed many of the native inhabitants of the Americas. European ships also carried the black rat to America and to other parts of the world, just as it had been carried by ship to Europe from Asia. The Norway rat also probably came to America by ship. Rat-borne diseases are believed to have taken more human lives in the last ten centuries than all the wars and revolutions ever fought. The unknown cargoes these ships carried from Europe brought far more tragedy than the known.

The English were naturally outdistanced in voyages of exploration by the older and wiser maritime nations of Spain and Portugal. However, in 1497 Henry VII granted John Cabot, an Italian living in London, the right to sail across the North Atlantic to find a route to the Orient. But the English king did not back this gesture with cash, and Cabot had to sail out of Bristol harbor on the *Mathew*, a vessel so small a writer of the time said it could hardly be called a "shippe." He had a small crew of eighteen on the *Mathew*, which was probably a sturdy little caravel of the time. In six weeks Cabot sighted North America. His most important discovery was not land but the fishing grounds of the North Atlantic which were already being worked by the hardy crews of Portuguese ships. However, this was the beginning of English exploration and settlement along the eastern Atlantic coast.

Until about 1450 both foreign and domestic trade goods were almost completely carried in ships of the Hanseatic League and other non-English ships. Then gradually the English began taking this trade into their own hands. In 1485 a law was passed stating that French wines must be imported in English ships and that the crews on these ships must be mainly English. It was in this same year, 1485, that Henry VII became king of England. He was the first of the incredible Tudor monarchs. A few years before, the English had lost all their possessions in France, except the port of Calais, as the aftermath of a war that had lasted a hundred years. England had also been plagued with revolts and civil strife. Henry VII realized that to make England strong and to establish law and order he had to have an army and navy; this required money. So he encouraged the export of wool in English ships, and English shipping began to grow.

A great Englishman named Bacon commented that Henry VII "could not endure to see trade sick." And for good reason, for by stimulating shipbuilding and trade the king collected money through taxes and "gifts" given him by courtiers and merchants to whom he granted trade monopolies. With the money, he had ships built to use in peace and war. His children thought him a miser because he would not spend money on fancy

John Cabot, 1451–1498.
From an unauthenticated Venetian painting.

The Mathew *skirting the Newfoundland shore,*
June 1797.

clothing and other finery. But the ships were expensive three- and four-masted craft that carried topsails, and even a third sail above that, a topgallant. For the price of a fine silk gown the king could buy fine sail, and the sail would help England much more than the showy gown.

Henry VII's ships were merchant warships, carracks armed with guns, except that now they belonged to the king and not to a merchant or to a seaport town from which they had to be impressed (impressment meant arrest) by the king when he needed warships. The English king was so determined to foster trade that he leased his warships to merchant syndicates for their longer voyages into the eastern Mediterranean. With these armed ships the chance of a safe voyage was increased. Also, the king turned a pretty penny from the deal.

The French kings at this time were encouraging commercial development on land more than on sea. The only sea trade the French were pursuing was in the eastern Mediterranean, where Turkish pirates were a great problem and where Venice barred the way for full French commercial development. In addition, so much trouble plagued the land that later became united as France that little energy was left for full participation in the boom of the period. And so, during the 1400s, France's maritime development was negligible.

At the same time, German shipping under the Hanseatic League was slowly going downhill. The Hanseatic League lost a good deal of its power when the herring fishing industry in the North Sea, which was controlled by Scotland, England, and Holland, became more profitable than the fishing in the German Baltic and around Sweden. The

reason for this had to do with the fish itself. During the 1400s the herring left the German fishing grounds and swam out into the North Sea. One very interesting theory as to why this happened is that the level of the water controlled by the Germans rose, and the herring, previously hindered by land barriers, were now able to swim out into the open sea. Whatever the reason, when the herring left they took much of the trade away from the Hanseatic League towns. The League was so worried about its loss of position that it prohibited the sale of ships outside the area. However, in the hope of immediate gain many of the German towns ignored the law. It is doubtful, even if the law had not been broken, whether German shipping would have been helped much, because by this time shipping centers in Europe were moving out along the rivers and coasts closer to the Atlantic.

The ocean was just beginning to open up. Long-distance shipping was becoming important. Still, in the 1400s most shipping was local, and most ships were small coastal and fishing vessels. The big galleys of Venice, the bulky carracks, and the trim caravels that crossed the ocean were the exceptions, not the rule. The smaller ports and the smaller ships were vastly in the majority. In a book published in 1486, a wonderful view of the harbor of Genoa shows small galleys; small coastal boats with single lateen sail; small, medium and fairly large cogs—all at anchor along with the larger carracks and the great merchant galleys.

These smaller ships did not head out into the Atlantic. They made only local trips. The casks of wine from some little-known vineyard would go to a small river port. A coaster would carry the casks to Bordeaux, perhaps, where they would be loaded onto a larger ship for the trip to London. In London the casks would be stored in a warehouse. When sold they were put onto a coastal ship to be forwarded to a smaller port. The casks might be sent overland, but if they were, the price of the wine would go up 15 to 20 percent, whereas if they went by ship the price would only be increased from 2 to 6 percent. (Now, centuries later, land transportation is still usually more costly than transportation by water.) In the case of very bulky cargoes, such as the low-priced grain of Prussia, shipment by sea—say to Holland—would increase the selling price by almost 50 percent. But if the grain had gone overland it would have cost its weight in gold.

By the end of the 1400s towns all over Europe were receiving goods from distant places. Even in smaller towns people were enjoying the taste of pepper and other spices. Inhabitants of the larger cities grew accustomed to grain and fish from other lands as a regular part of their diet. Most of the people still depended on the local mill to turn out the flour from local grain, and most of them still wore simple homespun clothes. But in case of famine, grain could be shipped in to be made into flour, and if a man were getting married and wanted a fancy shirt made from fine flaxen or woolen cloth manufactured in a distant country, the cloth would be available.

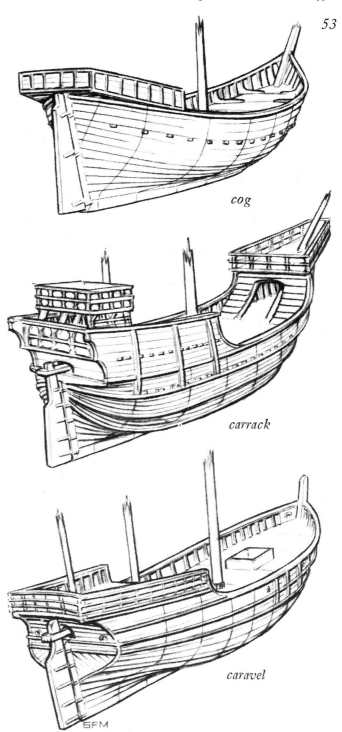

cog

carrack

caravel

Fifteenth-century hull types.

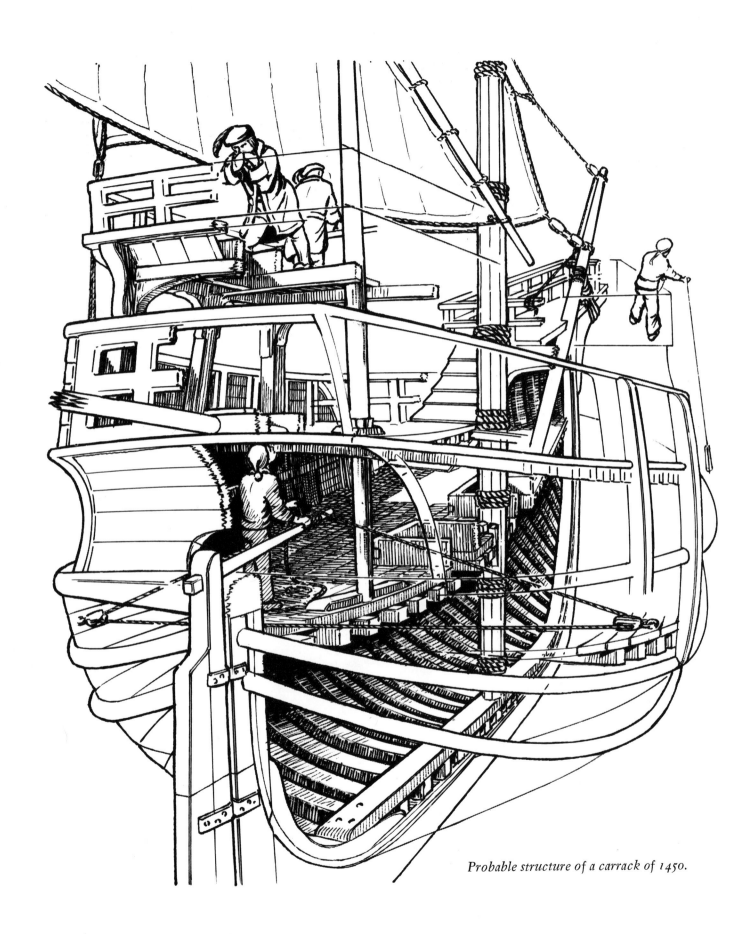

Probable structure of a carrack of 1450.

5.

Survival at Sea in the 1400s

LIFE aboard ship in the late 1400s was hard. Food was bad. Salt beef or salt fish made the men thirsty. The water to quench the thirst produced by such food was foul-tasting; seamen held their noses and closed their eyes before swallowing it. It smelled putrid and had small live creatures in it. And when the food ran out, as it often did, rats, mice, shoes and leather collars were eaten. On one voyage the seamen ate their pet monkeys and parrots. When these animals were gone they ate mice and rats. There were so many rattraps aboard that few rats were left alive, and those were hunted day and night. One man who had caught two rats was offered a new outfit of clothing from head to toe when the ship reached land if he would sell one of them. He did not accept, believing, and rightly, that if he sold the rat he might not be alive to receive the clothing later.

The seamen slept where they could: on deck, if possible; if not, below, where the air was suffocating. Sailors did begin sleeping in hammocks slung below deck after the discovery of the West Indies, where the Span-ish learned of their use from the Indians.

To work the sails and tend the ship called for many hands, and there was serious over-crowding aboard small ships. The work went on day and night. The men were on duty four hours and off four hours. When there was trouble no one slept. Tired, hungry, thirsty, wet, and too cold or too hot, a man had to be physically strong to survive these voyages.

But physical strength alone did not guar-antee completion of a long voyage, for scurvy was a common ailment. On very long voyages it might even kill most of the crew. Scurvy is a dietary disease caused by the lack of vitamin C, ordinarily obtained by eating fresh fruits and vegetables. Going without such foods for a few weeks could cause a man's body to swell; he would lose the use of his arms and legs; his teeth would fall out and his skin turn dark, often black. In the end, if vitamin C was not obtained by eating fresh food (vitamin pills were hun-dreds of years in the future), the man died.

Besides scurvy and death from injury, there was the constant threat of pirates.

56 There was really nothing romantic about pirates. They killed any man aboard a captured ship who would not join their crew. When they did not need new crew members they often murdered all the captives. If they did not kill the men outright they would set them afloat, without food or water, in a damaged ship which they made sure would not sail by taking the sails or by ripping them so that they could not be used. Then the men died a slow death.

On naval ships the laws of the sea were cruel: floggings were general, tar-and-feathering was common, sailors had their tongues cut out sometimes just for looking as if they were about to disobey an officer. And men who worked on the king's ships hardly ever knew how the ship's regulations were going to be carried out. One day the discipline would be so tight a man dared not look up from his work. Another day it would be so lax the crew would get drunk and not be punished.

Discipline on merchant ships and ships of exploration in the 1400s, however, was not nearly so severe as it later became. A merchant ship sailed by command of the captain and consent of the men. Crewmen received fair wages. Captains had to offer good pay to get seamen aboard ship in the first place. Besides his salary the crewman was often somewhat of a partner in the adventure: he received a portion of the profits at the end of a voyage if he was still alive. And, knowing how slim were their chances of surviving, men often would not sign on a ship without a contract guaranteeing that their share of the profits would go to their wives or families if they died. In this way a man would go to sea secure in the belief that

The helmsman's view, carrack of 1450.

Towing ship, 1470.

his family would be taken care of if he did not return. Sometimes sailors went on strike in port when they felt they were not being treated properly or receiving as much pay as they should. Even the powerful Doge of Venice knuckled under to the demands made by the pugnacious Venetian sailors.

Aboard ship, crew and captain worked hand in hand. The life of the ship and the success of the voyage depended on this cooperation. Columbus would have been compelled to turn back on his first voyage if the crew had insisted. And they almost did, for the men believed they were traveling before a steady wind that would never reverse and enable them to sail back to Spain. But Columbus persuaded them to journey on.

Some members of the crew had special jobs. The *boatswain* was the man in charge of the rigging and sails. He called the men to work with a chant or by blowing a whistle. In later usage the word boatswain meant the man in charge of discipline as well as of work. Another important member of the crew was the *caulker*. Caulking a ship means to force oakum (the loose fibers from old rope) into the ship's seams. This helps make a wooden ship watertight. The *cooper* aboard ship did just what the word suggests: he "cooped up" the food and water and made pens for any live animals that were taken aboard. The cooper's most important job was to make casks for carrying water, wine, and vinegar.

There were always young boys aboard ship. Some served the captain, running errands and carrying messages. Some served food to the men and helped in the galley, a place so filled with pots and pans the cook could hardly move around. Some had very

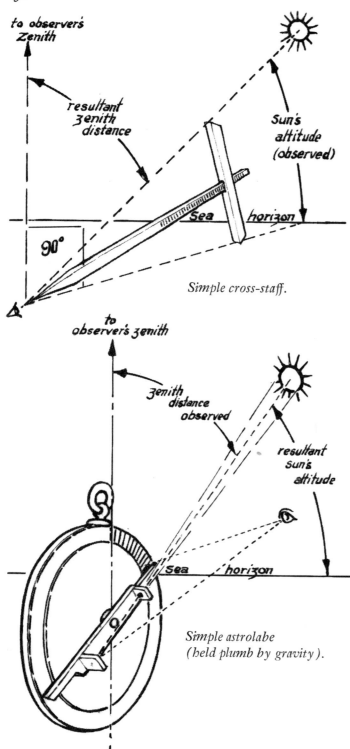

Simple cross-staff.

*Simple astrolabe
(held plumb by gravity).*

*Fifteenth-century instruments for measuring sun's
altitude.*

special and important jobs. One that must
have been dull but was very important was
turning the sandglass every half hour. Later
in the history of ships the sandglass was
turned every hour, and still later every four
hours, or, as the four-hour unit is called,
every watch.

Survival at sea depended on every man
doing his job, whether high on the yardarm
or manning the pump day after day; working watch on watch, or four, eight, sixteen
hours at a time in light and in darkness.
With numb hands, frozen clothing and con-
stantly waterlogged feet, the men of the
northern oceans scampered up the ratlines
and unfurled the sails. In the heat of the
tropics, itching with sweat and dizzy from
the constant glare of the sun, the men had
to man the oars on the ship's boat during
long periods of calm. Their hands raw and
their throats aching with thirst, they tried
in their small boat to pull the ship into a
wind, no matter how slight. It was a hard
and dangerous life. Sometimes the rewards were worth the risks, but often they
were not.

Navigation was accomplished with the
aid of crude instruments used to measure
the height of the sun. Once the position of
the sun is known, latitude can be judged.
One captain would use visual estimates in
gauging the position of the sun. Another
would use as a measuring stick so many
spans of his hand; still another, what in his
mind's eye was equal to the height of a man.
This vague way of measuring finally gave
way to the use of the *astrolabe,* a round instrument with an adjustable arm into which
peepholes were pierced. By moving the arms
until he could see the sun through the peepholes, a man could look at the scale of de-

grees on the disc and find out approximately where the ship was located in the ocean. At night the positions of the polestar in the north and the Southern Cross in the south were used to help navigate.

The *lead,* developed in northern waters to measure the depth of the water, was also helpful on voyages. A lead sinker was attached to a cord with various depths marked off on it. A seaman stood at the side of the ship, sometimes on a platform built out from the hull, dropped the lead, and when it reached bottom he sang off the depth. The lead was especially useful in unknown coastal waters. It was covered with tallow, to which samples of the bottom would cling. Probing or sounding the bottom of a strange strait or bay made it possible to avoid going aground. There were seamen so skillful in using the lead that they could sometimes tell from the kind of sand or mud below the ship whether it was heading for a bar or whether it would continue to run in the same depth of water for a long time.

The making of accurate maps and charts was developing rapidly. The Portuguese had *roterios,* books of sailing directions. They listed courses, distances and hazards, and included descriptions to aid in recognizing features of a coast. Such sailing directions were also called *portolani.* The maps that accompanied the *portolani* were called *portolan* maps. However, they did not show latitude or longitude; another bad feature was that certain areas were shown greatly out of proportion. The better known a place was, the larger it was drawn on the map. The less well known places were filled in only vaguely. At first these maps plotted the coasts of the Mediterranean and the Black Sea. Later they were enlarged to include the Atlantic and other parts of the world. Seamen found such maps helpful despite their inaccuracy.

But the guiding principles of navigation were still the same as those used by earlier seamen. Such navigation was called *dead reckoning.* With what help the compass and such crude instruments as the astrolabe offered, a captain headed off in a given direction, and as the days passed he simply guessed where he was and how much farther he had to go. Currents and wind direction were taken into consideration, but none of these gauges were ever really dependable. However, if, for instance, a ship sailed in the general direction of the West Indies or of South or North America, it was hard to miss them. Columbus sailed from the Canaries on his first voyage. On his second voyage he sailed from the Azores. He reached the West Indies both times by dead reckoning. He did not reach the same place twice, but he did arrive in the same general area, and in those days that was all a navigator could hope for.

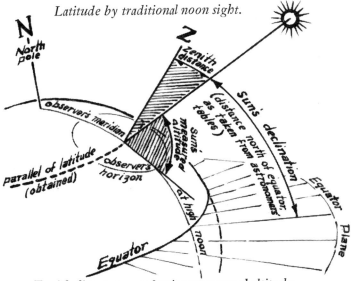

Latitude by traditional noon sight.

Zenith distance = 90° minus measured altitude.
Latitude = sun's declination plus zenith distance.

Carracks of 1500 grappled together for hand-to-hand combat.

Gun barrel made from fused iron rods.

6.
The Magnificent Galleon

THE 1500s were marked by adventure at sea. Kings built great ships of war and merchants built great ships for trade. Explorers went to the ice-packed Arctic seeking a northern passage to the Orient. Men sailed around the world and brought home fortunes in treasure. On one exciting French voyage a cure for scurvy was discovered and then, incredibly, forgotten. Fleets of galleys fought furious battles. The Manila Galleons of Spain began their famous and envied voyages across the Pacific carrying back the riches of the Orient, and it became the dream of many seamen to capture one of the galleons and live like a rajah for the rest of his life.

The ships in which men sailed were carrack men-of-war and merchantmen of all sizes; galleons, galleys, galleasses; gigantic caravels as well as small ones; plus coastal fore-and-aft-rigged craft. Ships became bigger and carried more *top-hamper*—the weight aloft of masts, yards, rigging and sail. The hulls of the large northern ships were carvel-built now rather than clinker-built. This gave them a stronger body. Ships which at the beginning of the 1500s looked cumbersome and top-heavy had a cleaner line and look by the end of the century.

The carrack, which was used as a merchant ship for long hauls for years to come, continued to change. In the early 1500s the towering castles, sometimes four or five decks high aft and two or three decks high at the prow, were built into these ships so that the decks could carry fighting men and guns. The more decks, the more guns. But then a Frenchman came up with a different idea, a better one: Why not put the guns belowdeck and cut holes in the side of the ship through which the guns could fire? It proved to be such a good idea that most guns remained belowdeck until sailing warships became obsolete. Heavy cannon firing through gunports along the length of the deck allowed a ship to deliver shot from stem to stern, giving the enemy a broadside volley and not merely a scattering of shot from various areas.

With the development of broadside firing and the improvement of cannon an enemy could be put out of action at a distance. No

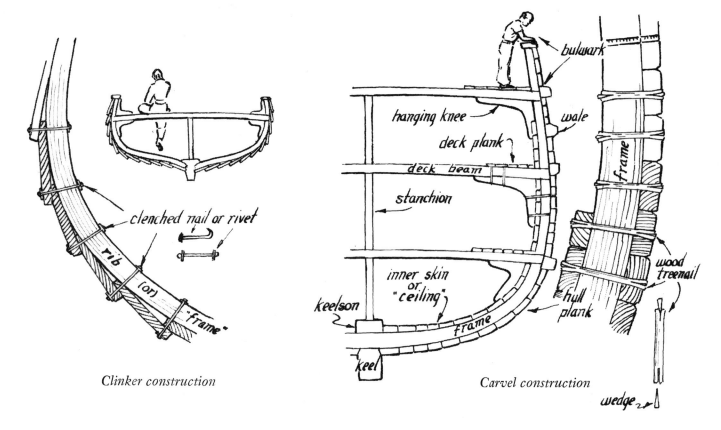

Clinker construction

Carvel construction

longer was it necessary to board and fight hand to hand to capture and defeat an enemy ship. Boarding and fighting hand to hand did not disappear from naval warfare, but it diminished in importance through the years as cannon became heavier and more effective. The enormous forecastle projecting over the bow in the large carracks became a less desirable feature, and the grand heights of the aftercastle slowly dwindled to more practical proportions as the century wore on. Broadside firing brought the warship into its own, and from the 1500s onward warships were built for the single purpose of carrying guns and fighting crews. Merchant ships carrying guns did not go out of existence, but they were not used so often as out-and-out fighting ships. Still, a merchant seaman had to know gunnery as well as the ropes. Pirates and privateers were

always eager to capture rich cargoes. Guns remained aboard merchant vessels even when national navies with powerful warships could offer safe passage over certain sea routes.

What is generally thought of as the famous Spanish galleon, which has been so often written about romantically, made its appearance in the 1500s. Like a mushroom, it seems to have sprung full blown into existence overnight. Italy, Spain and Portugal all seem to have built galleons for ocean voyages in the first half of the century. The first great galleon built by the city of Venice for use on the ocean was constructed in the 1520s. The carrack was a blending of the round and the long ships of ancient times, but, favoring the round ship, it was broad of beam, and it grew broader as it grew older. The galleon was also a joining of round and long ships; however, galleons tended to favor long ships such as the galley. At first the galleon was narrow and fast, small and maneuverable. The superstructure of the forecastle did not project over the bow as it did in the carrack, but was placed farther back, and the bow was built out. A large pointed ram-like structure called the *beak,* and later the *beakhead,* was added. The stern was not round but flat, as in earlier caravels. Sterns that are flat and do not come to a point are called square-ended, even, oddly enough, when the end is not really square.

As did most of the large ships of the time, the galleon had four masts. At first the foremast was set in front of the forecastle; later it was moved back somewhat and poked up through the deck of the forecastle itself. The mainmast was set in front of the quar-

terdeck, and the mizzenmast in front of the poop deck. (*Puppis* was the Roman word for stern, and the French used it—*poupe*—to denote the stern and also the highest deck aft. The word came into English usage about 1500.) The bonaventure mizzenmast was set up through the poop deck itself. The smaller galleons, however, had only three masts, the bonaventure mizzen being omitted. Later on, large galleons adopted this three-masted style.

The galleon's sails were square on foremast and mainmast. The spritsail was also square. The sails on the mizzen and bonaventure mizzen were lateen. Sails were no longer simply square, although they were still called square sails. The first sail above the deck was square, or very squarishly rectangular, but the topsail and topgallant were wider at the bottom than at the top. This cut

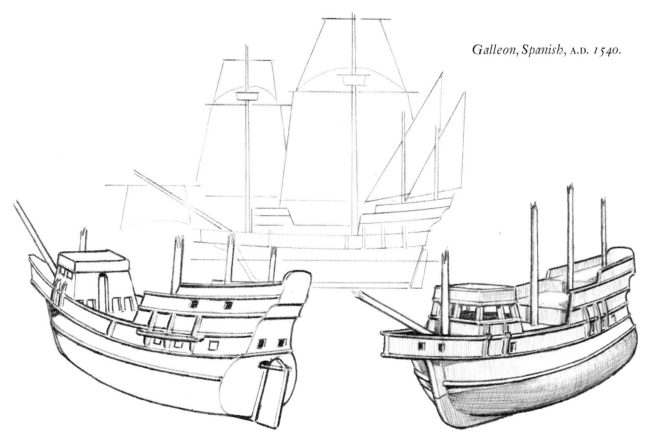

Galleon, Spanish, A.D. *1540.*

down on the size of the yards, and in turn reduced the weight that the narrower part of the mast had to carry. It was in this period that sails became broader. In some ships the mainsail was truly enormous, extending a long way out from the sides of the ship.

Galleons did not, of course, spring up overnight, even though that may seem to be the case in light of their sudden appearance in paintings and models. The Italians had been building ships with galleon-like features for many years. Their galleon-like galley was designed to travel under sail alone or with both sail and oar. One Italian ship built in the 1400s, the *barza,* had a bow very much like the galleon. Small oared galleonlike ships called *galeoni* were built for use on rivers. Portugal and Spain had similar ships. But no "glory" accompanied these smaller locally used ships; they were not painted by the artists at the king's court, and they were ignored by writers intent on impressing rich merchants with the greatness of their large cargo fleets.

As the galleon and other fast ships were coming into general use the galley was declining in importance, even though the Arsenal in Venice produced many of them during the 1500s. The fate of the galley parallels that of the sailing ship: the beauty of its design and construction reached its greatest heights just as the type of ship itself was being replaced by more efficient vessels. Square-rigged ships replaced galleys as passenger ships for pilgrims to the Holy Land during the early 1500s. They also replaced galleys for carrying the rich cargoes of the south. And although galleys were used as warships against each other for many years, and very beautiful galleys were

made in France until 1720, the galleon eventually replaced them as the principal warship in Europe.

But before the galley was replaced as a fighting ship, the great sea battle of Lepanto took place in 1571. The Turks had become a power in the Mediterranean in the 1400s, and Turkish raids and piracy were an unending threat to all the countries using these waters. It looked as if the Turks were about to take over that inland sea. So the navies of the Italian cities, with some help from Spain, decided to meet the Turks in battle. Don Juan of Austria, a courageous young man, commanded over 200 galleys for the Europeans. The Turks under the command of Ali Pasha also had more than 200 galleys. Experience and skill were in the Turks' favor, for the Turkish fleet was a well established and coordinated unit.

When the battle of Lepanto began both sides attacked furiously. The six large ships leading the European fleet began their powerful bombardment and caused the Turkish galleys a great deal of damage. The crescent line of battle in which the Turkish armada was attacking was broken up. In the hand-to-hand fighting that followed, Don Juan killed Ali Pasha. The Europeans gained an astounding victory. Twelve thousand Christian galley slaves who had been serving aboard Turkish ships were freed. The battle had lasted only four hours, but thousands of men had died, and for the time being, Turkish control of the Mediterranean was crushed. But two years later Venice was forced to deliver the strategic island of Cyprus to the Turks. Her wars with the Turks helped to weaken Venice, and her importance as a sea power declined.

The deciding factors in the victory at Le-

Lepanto, October 7, 1571; Christians vs. Turks.
456 vessels engaged. 60,000 rowers.
Twilight of galley warfare.

Venetian galleass.
Mid-1500s.

panto were many, among them, the intelligent leadership of Don Juan of Austria, the overconfidence of the Turks, and the use of the six ships that gave the Turkish galleys such a terrible pounding. These ships were galleasses, or great galleys that had been designed exclusively for war, with no thought of trade. Heavier, larger, and loaded with guns, they were distinct from other galleys. The sides were higher, which made the ship more difficult to board. Both oars and triangular lateen sails were used, and a powerful ram, reinforced with metal, jutted from a prow equipped with many guns.

Spain, Italy and France put the galleasses to good use for many years. The north tried to make use of them also, but designed them differently. Theirs were long, low ships with square sail and fitted for rowing. They proved not to be effective in northern waters and were soon eliminated from service.

The Venetian and French galleasses and galleys were truly beautiful ships. But by the 1500s crews were no longer made up of free men. Galley slaves were chained in position at the oars and were flogged to goad them into rowing faster. The odor from these ships was suffocatingly foul, and northern sailors did not like to get within smelling distance. However, there was little need, for one square-rigged ship could defeat a number of galleys. There are instances of lone square-rigged ships winning battles against as many as thirty-five galleys. With such decisive victories credited to square-rigged warships it is no wonder that the days of the oared long ship were numbered.

Another memorable battle of the 1500s took place in the English Channel. In 1588 a large Spanish fleet was sent to escort and protect an invading army based at Dunkirk for an attack on England across the Channel. It was only seventeen years after Lepanto, but there is a striking difference in the ships used in this battle. Here galleon fought against galleon. The English galleons were small and streamlined, with castles lowered and keel lengthened. The lines (the contour of a vessel) of these ships were, in general, the lines of fighting ships for the next few centuries with only slight modifications.

The fleets of the English and the Spanish were an interesting contrast. The Spanish galleons were large and cumbersome, heavily laden with guns, sailors and soldiers. The smaller English galleons were fast and easier to handle; the crews were not nearly so large, and the ship's decks were unencumbered with troops. Accompanying their galleons the Spanish used galleasses and galleys, but both were dismal failures in the choppy Channel. In addition to their galleons the English used both a smaller privateer-type galleon and merchant ships equipped with guns, and these were most effective.

The Spanish fleet was a wonderful sight, ranged in beautiful formation, but deployed as if the ships were units of horse and infantry. The English ships did not engage in a direct encounter with the Spanish ships. Instead, they sailed along the rear of the Spanish formation, fired, then came about and repeated the maneuver. They used a rough sort of line-of-battle formation, nipping and using their broadsides as often as possible. As one Spaniard said after the battle: "We saw how, by the use of very

The Spanish Armada off Plymouth, England, June 21, 1588. The English use of cannon was decisive.

good and very light ships, it was possible for them to come and go any way they pleased which we could not do." The English ships were not successful in deterring the Spaniards, nor did they inflict heavy damage, but on the sea theirs was a fairly new tactic, the forerunner of the naval line-of-battle which the Dutch developed into an art during the next century. With poor organization, the weather against them, and the harassment by the English, the Spanish fleet broke up. Philip II, king of Spain, wrote: "The uncertainty of naval enterprises is well known."

Both the English and the Spanish used a ship called a *pinnace* during this protracted encounter. As is often the case, the name was used for more than one type of small craft. In England it meant anything from a large rowboat to a small sailing vessel of fifty to eighty tons with auxiliary oars and guns. At the end of the 1500s the Dutch built a pinnace-type ship that was high, flat-sterned and full-rigged. To confuse the matter more, row-barges were sometimes called pinnaces. In the case of the Spanish,

the pinnaces were used for scouting and sending messages between the fleet and the shore, as well as between ships. They were probably small, light two-masted ships, flat-sterned, with a single deck.

Small and medium-sized ships were used extensively for trade and exploration during this century. Exploration often—but not always—brought rich rewards in trade monopolies. It also helped give the European an idea of his geographic position in a world much larger and more varied than he had suspected. But still the European believed himself not only at the center of the universe, but at the very heart of the world. This mistaken attitude stemmed from the fact that he was able to control the development of the people and raw materials in most of the lands that his ships reached. The efficient use of the sailing ship enabled him to transport troops for conquest. Large and deadly navies allowed European countries to dictate to less well developed nations how the oceans would be used. In controlling the trade of these countries, these European nations kept

Detail from a contemporary woodcut representing the battle of Malacca Strait, 1602. These two Dutch vessels attacking the large Portuguese carrack are probably pinnaces.

Juan Sebastian del Cano— from the sculpture at Guetaria, Spain.

Ferdinand Magellan, 1480–1521, from a sixteenth-century engraving.

October 1520. The Strait of Magellan.

much of the world from advancing industrially. "Sea power" is not an empty phrase. It was with ships that Europe colonized and conquered. It was with ships of trade and war that the colonies were forced to supply raw materials, food, and even luxury items to the countries of Europe.

A small Spanish *noa*, a type of carrack that in stormy weather rolled over so far that its yardarms touched the water, was the first ship to sail around the world. This ship's name was *Vittoria*, and for three years its crew fought ocean and wind—and more—to bring her back to Spain, from which she had sailed in 1519. The *Vittoria*

sailed with four other carrack-type ships under the command of a Portuguese navigator, Ferdinand Magellan. The Spanish captains accompanying Magellan planned, even before leaving port, to kill this foreigner, who led the expedition on a ship called the *Trinidad*. They tried twice. On the second try Magellan (very sensibly) had one of them beheaded and another marooned on the coast of South America. Then one of the ships was wrecked. The other four sailed on through freezing storms to find the strait that would carry the ships into the Pacific. Another of the ships sneaked away and sailed back to Spain. When Magellan did find the strait, five weeks of backbreaking work followed to get the three remaining vessels through the dangerous passage. Snow-covered mountains rose on both sides. Below, the water was treacherously swift. Some sections were so narrow it seemed impossible to pass without having the ships broken to splinters against the high stone cliffs.

Once in the Pacific they sailed for months before coming to an island where they could find food and fresh water. They ate what leather there was aboard to keep alive. Nineteen men died of scurvy; the rest were so weak they could hardly sail the ships. Finally, in March of 1521, they reached the Philippines. Magellan made trade agreements and converted the king of Cebu, one of the islands in the group, and his people to the Christian faith. And there, in the Philippines, Magellan was speared to death in an attempt to conquer the island of Mactan. The three ships continued the voyage without their commander. One had to be dismantled and burned because it was no longer able to navigate. Another ship, whose mainmast had been blown off by high winds, had only nineteen men left, out of a crew of fifty-four, and these were ill. She was captured by the Portuguese, and only three men aboard ever returned to Spain.

The *Vittoria* sailed on, rounded the Cape of Good Hope and arrived in Spain almost exactly three years from the day she had left. Out of a fleet of five ships with 280 men, one ship and 18 men returned. Sebastian del Cano was the first captain to sail around the world. But it was Magellan who had opened the Philippines to Spain. A new route, the long one from the East Indies and China to the Philippines to South America and then to Europe, had been proved possible. In 1565 the famous Manila Galleons of Spain began crossing the Pacific. The treasures of the Orient—silks, gems and porcelain from China, the spices of the East Indies—reached Spain by this route for two centuries. The galleons sailed between Manila in the Philippines and Acapulco on the west coast of Mexico. The treasure gathered by ships in the Pacific was sent overland and added to the silver and gold mined or collected in America; it was then put on ships of the Spanish treasure fleet which shuttled back and forth between the Old and New World. A curious sidelight into this shipment of treasure was that the silver and gold coins were often shipped in jars of pitch to prevent their being stolen by anyone aboard. Perhaps that's where the expression "sticky fingers" originated.

Francis Drake, an Englishman, circumnavigated the globe later in the century. His was the first English exploit in the Pacific, and it brought treasure and fame to Drake and acclaim for his ship, the *Pelican*, which, with good reason, he later renamed the *Golden Hind*. Drake's ship was a *bark*. The term "bark," like "pinnace," was applied to a variety of ships: ships that were rowed on rivers, ships used in the wine trade, and others. Drake's bark carried topgallant sails on main and foremast, so it must have been a large one. The ship had fourteen gunports through which bronze cannon could blaze.

Drake's voyage was well organized. He sailed away with viol players and trumpeters aboard. His men liked and respected him, and there was little worry about mutiny, even though Drake lived in high style.

Plymouth

Golden Hind—*her only known picture.*
Detail from an early seventeenth-century
map by Jacob Hondius.

Sir Francis Drake, 1540–1596,
after the engraving by Houbraken.

SFM

He captured a Spanish ship with a rich cargo in January 1578 off the Cape Verde Islands, less than a month after sailing. He crossed over to Brazil and, after two weeks' rest, passed down the coast and through the Straits of Magellan. It took only two weeks to get into the Pacific. Off Valparaiso another Spanish ship carrying wine and gold was captured, then a ship with silver and coin. Out of Callao, the port to Lima, he gave chase to another treasure ship. By fortunate timing and some determined sailing he caught this ship and ordered surrender. The master laughed and called back: "What old tub orders me to strike sail? Come aboard and do it yourself!" Drake and his crew did just that, and took gold, silver and coins to the tune of a king's ransom. Next, they sacked the town of Guatulco in Mexico.

Drake's movements during the following weeks are not known with any certainty. He may have stopped somewhere along the California coast and sailed even farther north. If this was the case, he might have been searching for a short route back to England. The legend of a northwest passage through the ice fields was popular in Europe at that time. Not finding the passage, Drake may have decided to follow the Spanish example and cross the Pacific. In any case, he stopped and overhauled his ship, then headed into the Pacific. He got food and water in the Polynesian islands and sailed on to Tenato. There he traded with the sultan, buying six tons of cloves, three tons of which had to be heaved overboard when the ship caught on a rock going through the Celebes. Miraculously, the ship freed itself without damage. Then he sailed to the Cape of Good Hope and

home to a hero's welcome at Portsmouth in September 1580.

Drake's haul was rich beyond imagining. Queen Elizabeth I knighted him in 1581 because of this adventure. Many in Europe cheered, but the Spanish government protested this unlawful privateering venture that had taken place in peacetime, especially since it was so openly approved by the devious queen of England. Drake, however, brought more than gold and silver to England. He was a remarkable observer. He accurately recorded navigational and geographic information. He studied Portuguese sea routes, ports and defenses. He took note of trees, birds, sea lions and other creatures and painted their pictures. His voyage, besides being a personal success, was the opening phase of English penetration into the East. While Drake was cheered in the streets, merchants and seamen pored over his charts and data in paneled offices and dockside taverns. Drake's adventures made even the most timid individuals want to board a ship and head for the Indies. Many men did just that, and within twenty years the English East India Company had begun its profitable history.

Drake's voyage on the *Golden Hind* had the touch of a lark to it and ended in a flare of glory. But a voyage made by a young man born in 1563 in Haarlem, Holland, made as much of a stir amongst the Dutch as Drake's voyage had created in England. Jan Huygen van Linschoten's story is one of the most fascinating ever told. At sixteen van Linschoten shipped from the Netherlands as a cabin boy. He sailed for Spain, the very country from whom the Low Countries were fighting to be free. Dutch ships were winning the war against Spanish ships, but her soldiers were losing to Spanish troops on land. Money was needed to keep the army fighting, and, incredibly, the Dutch went to Spain to get the money. They could do this because they controlled the grain shipments of Europe, and although gold and silver poured into Spanish harbors, grain did not. Without grain the Spanish at home went hungry, so although they were at war with the Netherlands, the Spanish had to buy their grain from the Dutch. (Dutch ships had to declare themselves another nationality, but everyone accepted the subterfuge.) With the gold that Spain paid them for their grain, the Dutch bought supplies to fight the Spanish army. And eventually they were victorious.

Young Jan Huygen van Linschoten knew he was helping his country on this voyage to Spain. He realized that he could help more if he learned Spanish secrets concerning their ships. He had been in Spain only a short time when a friend suggested he go to Lisbon to get information about the Spaniards there, for Portugal had just been taken over by the king of Spain. He lived in Lisbon for three years, and when he was twenty, in 1583, he sailed for Goa in India in the position of secretary to the Portuguese archbishop of Goa.

He traveled on a ship that was part of a fleet of forty bound for India. When the navigators' observations seemed to indicate that the ships had rounded the Cape of Good Hope, they had actually passed it several days earlier. This is a good example of the sort of error in navigation that was common in the sixteenth century. After five months at sea van Linschoten arrived at Goa. On this voyage only thirty men had

died, a very good record for that day and age.

When the archbishop died in 1589, van Linschoten, having lived among the Portuguese for six years, headed home to the Netherlands. During his stay he had learned the secrets of Portuguese trade. What he saw convinced him that the Dutch were better seamen and traders. Inefficient and careless practices prevailed among the Portuguese, and corruption was common on the docks in Goa. If a shipper did not pay graft at dockside, his bales and bags of merchandise were left on the dock in all weather, or poorly stowed when taken on board. The decks on homeward-bound ships were piled so high with boxes, bales and crates that the sailors had little room to work. When van Linschoten's ship was only a few days out of port a boy fell overboard. The sea was calm, and rescuing him should have been a simple matter. But the boy drowned because the ship's boat was so loaded with boxes the crew could not lower it in time. Later in the voyage to lighten the ship during a storm this boat with all its boxes was cut away and lost.

On its trip homeward van Linschoten's ship fell in with another going to Europe. The captains decided to race around the Cape of Good Hope. The other ship took the lead as a storm came up, and when it cleared, the bodies and wreckage floating on the water told those aboard van Linschoten's ship what had happened to their racing partner. In another storm the ship's rudder broke. The Portuguese had been so eager for cargo they had not brought along the heavy anvil with which they could easily have repaired the damage. However, they did find a way to patch it.

Because of the poor diet on the long voy-

74   age, those aboard the ship grew sick. At St. Helena they stopped and ate fresh food, goats, wild pigs, and pigeons. Such island stops were necessary to fight scurvy, and every country with a large merchant fleet tried to control as many of them as possible along a trade route. Jan van Linschoten's ship sailed out of St. Helena leaving the sickest sailors behind. Still, ten more men died as the ship sailed north to the Azores.

At the Azores the captain and crew went ashore, leaving only the cabin boys and slaves to look after the ship. When a storm came up during the night the ship was thrown against others in the harbor, smashed to pieces and sunk. In the morning the shore was littered with silk and bales of spices. The ship on which van Linschoten finally reached home was almost sunk in a collision with another ship at sea. Then, within sight of the Netherlands, the ship was again nearly wrecked. This voyage shows how risky life aboard a carrack-type cargo ship was in the 1500s.

After the voyage van Linschoten, although a young man, became the consulting pilot to Dutch merchants. While working at this job he wrote the story of his stay in India. His book was eagerly read by the Dutch because he had actually been over the Portuguese sea route to the Orient and knew about the Portuguese trade in detail. It became the handbook for Dutch navigators going to the East Indies. Soon after it was written they were able to break the Portuguese monopoly in the East. The efficient Dutch reaped a rich harvest. Within a few years the Dutch government established the famous Dutch East India Company to handle the trade.

Dutch and English competition hurt Por-
tuguese shipping in the East. But Portugal was losing her position as a great sea power for another reason. She was too small and underpopulated to keep her trade routes for herself. As the Portuguese poet de Camões wrote: "Oh, my beloved sons, why venture out on the cruel sea which will surely become your shroud? Why go so far in search of foes, when the enemy rages at your gates? You may be Lords of India, Persia, Arabia and Ethiopia; but what do these titles avail you when your ancient kingdom is left depopulated, weakened and ruined? Heaven curse the man who first launched timber onto the sea or first unfurled a sail!" Poets, kings and seamen in other countries were to curse sea, ship and sail in years to come.

The history of ships during the 1500s is an exciting one. England, a country that had bought ships from other countries or used foreign shipwrights to build them at home, was by the end of the century building her own ships with her own shipwrights. Many of these ships were gigantic, having six decks and fitted with as many as 184 guns. English trade also took long strides forward during the sixteenth century. By 1598 the country had advanced to such a degree that the once powerful Hanseatic League was expelled from London. The English had their own East India Company, and they established a company to deal with trade in the Levant as well.

English and Dutch ships had begun to cover the globe, and Spanish ships were already carrying the treasures of the world to Spain. But Spain's ships were no longer built in the Mediterranean. When Spain wanted to rebuild its fleet in 1597, the galleons were bought from her former subjects

Dockyard activity, Holland,
late 1500s.

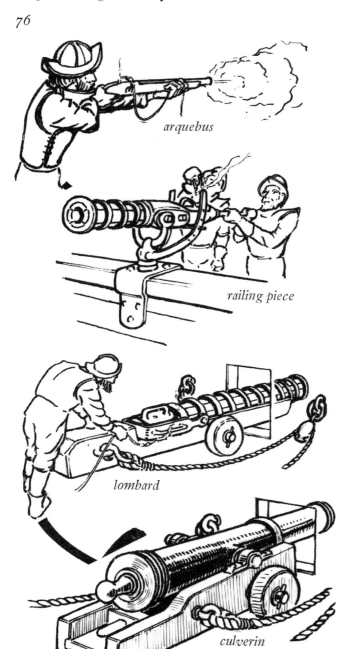

arquebus

railing piece

lombard

culverin

Sixteenth-century shipboard firearms.

Spanish government much, for mining in the New World was carried on by private interests. The king received only a small percentage of the precious metals imported into the country. In general, Spain was a very poor country, chiefly because of the continual encouragement of sheep-raising, which resulted in soil erosion due to overgrazing. Food was scarce because not enough of the land was put to more suitable and productive agricultural use, and most of the population went hungry. Also, the resources of the Spanish government were taxed by continual wars with France, England, and the Low Countries. Time after time Spanish victories on land were counterbalanced by defeat at sea. Because of her economic policies and these wars, the riches that came in went out as fast. By the end of the century Spain was deeply in debt. Portuguese and Spanish power at sea was passing to the Dutch and English. Spanish power on land passed to France, whose sea power was limited because she traded mostly with her European neighbors by land. Also, French overseas colonies were not yet successful enough to call for an expensive oceanic fleet.

It was during this century that the port of Antwerp in what is today Belgium became the center of sea trade. Each week at least fifty merchant ships sailed into Antwerp harbor, not counting the nearly one thousand fishing boats. There were a thousand business houses to handle this enormous trade. But in 1576 Antwerp was sacked by Spain, and Antwerp as a seaport never recovered. The ships moved to Amsterdam and London. The stage was set for wars of empire and the struggle for supremacy at sea.

in the Low Countries. By the mid-1500s Spanish colonists in America began developing vast ranches and plantations so that these colonies could become less dependent on gold and silver alone for survival. In any case, the gold and silver did not help the

Galleons, late 1500s.
Cannon had become the primary shipboard armament.

English galleon, late 1500s.

7

Aristocrats Aboard Ship

"THE LIFE at sea is the life for me" is a line from a song about the sea, but taking a look aboard ship in the sixteenth century might cause a person to sing a different tune. The lot of the seaman grew worse and worse as ships became larger and more complex. Discipline in a wartime navy had always been harsh; now it grew even more so. The laws of the sea dating from ancient times were set down in England in the early 1300s. These laws were enlarged upon in France and became stricter. Floggings, even for such a simple offense as swearing, were everyday affairs, and deaths from flogging were common. The punishments imposed aboard naval ships were gradually introduced aboard merchant ships as well.

The captains aboard the king's ships were usually aristocrats. In general they ignored the basic needs of the men under their command, and they were confident that their decisions were infallible—not a very good combination aboard a ship. On merchant ships, too, the captain was often a member of the upper class. The master,

not the captain, was in charge of cargo and the details concerning trade. The helmsman was responsible for navigation and for the care of the rudder and foremast, the two parts of the ship essential for navigating. The helmsman's assistant, the boatswain, came into his own as the working executive officer of the ship. He was in command of the crew, and he in turn had an assistant, the master-at-arms, who administered punishment. The master-at-arms was in charge of the guards who served as the ship's police force. And so on down the line of steward, carpenter, and caulker, each with his special job. The constable was in charge of working the gun crews. The lowest orders of men aboard ship were the first-class seamen, the common seamen and the apprentices.

The ship's barber was in charge of hygiene. He was also the ship's physician and surgeon, for although there were skilled doctors of medicine at the time, and great surgeons, they rarely went to sea. On a ship the barber treated the seamen just as he treated his patients ashore. A barber

Ship's doctor, 1500s.

shop was not only a place where shaves and haircuts were given, but also a place where people were bled; bleeding was thought to be the cure for many sicknesses. For instance, a pint of blood was drawn from a person every few days if he or she suffered from deep melancholy, which of course is a mental illness. Or a bowl of blood was taken twice a day from a person suffering with lung trouble. Gradually barbers began to stock medicines to cure headaches, the flux (which meant anything from hemorrhaging to dysentery), and other ailments. They were also called on to set bones and treat wounds. It was a legal and honorable trade, but filled with humbug, and the barber's services were often fatal.

Aboard ship, barbers were not very highly thought of, but most countries had laws which made it impossible for a ship to clear port unless there was a doctor of some sort aboard.

The days when the captain and crew worked hand in hand were fast disappearing. The position of the captain aboard ship began to take on the aura of godlike dominance which it held for many centuries afterward. The reason was simple: the king and his nobles had come to believe that their right to rule over others came to them directly from a divine power. Whether on land or sea, a nobleman never doubted that he was one of the chosen. It seemed perfectly reasonable to these aristocrat-captains that their power to rule was as absolute at sea as on their estates ashore. It is an interesting fact that the seamen themselves seldom questioned their own totally inferior position until very late in the 1700s.

While the lot of the seaman was growing harsher, the ships themselves, due to improved rigging and design, were becoming more dependable craft. Navigating at sea became somewhat simpler with the introduction of the *whipstaff*. Up to this time the steersman, standing below the deck and taking orders from above, had guided the rudder by operating a wooden bar attached to it; the bar is called a *tiller*. The whipstaff was an upright pole or lever that pivoted in the deck, the lower end secured to the fore end of a tiller. This enabled the steersman to stand on the deck in the open where he could watch the sails and note the direction in which the wind was blowing. The rudder could be adjusted by moving the whipstaff, which moved the tiller, which in turn moved the rudder.

Navigation still depended mainly on the lead, the lookout, and the determination of latitude. The use of the log (an actual log, not a written one) to measure the speed of a ship became common in the 1500s. The log was thrown from the bow of the ship, and the time required for it to float even with the stern was recorded; from this the ship's speed could be roughly calculated. The log as a means of measuring speed was replaced by a line in which knots were tied about 49 feet apart. This line was lowered into the water and after half a minute had passed a sailor checked to see which knot had been reached. This gave the speed, or knots, in nautical miles.

Whipstaff.

Dutch galleon of 1626.

8.
The Dutch:
Seamen Extraordinary

DURING the 1600s when Rembrandt was painting his masterpieces in Holland, a patient, methodical Dutch explorer named Abel Tasman was searching the southern Pacific for a mythical continent reputed to be the richest place in the world. And while Sir Christopher Wren, an English architect, was designing his famous churches to replace those destroyed in the great fire of London, slaves and free men were being carried across oceans to work the English plantation colonies. Great artists such as Rembrandt and Wren went peacefully about their business while Europe was in a state of almost continual war and revolution. During these dramatic times large fighting fleets, with ships-of-the-line, their guns roaring, came into existence. Merchant ships raced to Java and Japan (open only to the Dutch) carrying "unicorn horns" and gallstones of oxen to trade for silver and gold, cinnamon and ginger. Manhattan Indians watched working yachts sail the Hudson River, yachts that were very different from the ones we see today on that same river, over three hundred years later.

During the 1600s France became the leading power in Europe. To create a new fleet the French ordered ships built in Dutch shipyards. One of these, depicted in 1626 by a Dutch engraver, Hendrik Hondius, clearly shows the type of man-of-war used by European countries at that time. Hondius's ship was a galleon. Most larger ships, especially the men-of-war, were built along galleon lines until late in the 1700s. The new features on this ship were a spritsail topsail and a square mizzen topsail. The spritsail topsail was carried at the end of the bowsprit on a small mast which had evolved from a flagpole. Gratings had replaced the solid planking on the forecastle deck; other decks also had gratings to provide an outlet for the smoke created by the blasting of cannon.

The Hondius ship was three-masted. In fact, nearly all large vessels now were being built with three masts, a practice that would continue until sailing ships were forced off the sea by steamships. The draw-

84 ing also shows ornate galleries and decorations. The galleries were a new feature at the galleon's stern. In the late 1500s platforms which served the officers as a lavatory were built onto the stern of many ships. (The crewmen used the beakhead. The latrine on naval ships today is still called the *head,* a reminder of where lavatories were originally located.) Later on, the size of the stern balcony was increased and a portion covered and enclosed where the lavatory was located. The rest of the balcony was used by the officers for relaxing in the open, out of sight of the men. The officers found the balconies so enjoyable that soon two and even three were built onto the stern. When they were completely covered they became the ship's galleries. In the seventeenth century, galleries were heavily decorated, some with cupolas, windows and elaborate carvings. But by the end of the century, as ships became more efficient fighting vessels, the carved doodads began to disappear. Some had, in fact,

grown so elaborate and clumsy that they interfered with the handling of a ship under sail. Finally the galleries were totally incorporated into the stern, and much of the decoration was done away with.

The Swedish ship *Vasa,* a galleon built in 1627 (one year following Hondius's drawing of the Dutch ship), gives us a fine example of the ornate carvings and decorations used on ships built in that period. The *Vasa,* which sank in Stockholm harbor, was brought up from the depths in 1961. Splendidly carved animals and gods and goddesses of ancient times adorned its prow and stern. The *Vasa* was richly gilded and covered with bright colors, as were many ships before the advantages of camouflage were recognized.

The galleon *Vasa* sank in 1628 as it began its maiden voyage. A sudden squall came up and this magnificent-looking ship heeled over. Though it looked grand, it was too narrow and sharp at bottom, and not enough space had been provided for suffi-

Stern galleries.

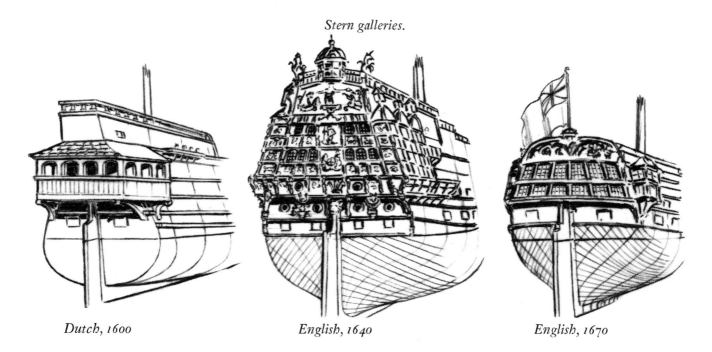

Dutch, 1600   *English, 1640*   *English, 1670*

Ship's head, Dutch, after 1650.

cient ballast. The ballast was generally of stone. Brick was sometimes used in ships traveling to undeveloped areas, the ship's ballast then being used to build houses. In later years iron bars were used and proved to be more convenient for loading and unloading. Ballast at the bottom of the ship keeps it on an even keel, settling the ship down in the water to a level that helps prevent it from capsizing. Built as it was, if the *Vasa* had carried as much ballast as it really needed, the ship's gunports would have been below water. Ships right through the 1800s often were built with their gunports so near the water that sometimes in rapid maneuvering it was impossible to close them fast enough to avoid flooding and sinking.

The sinking of the *Vasa* was considered a great misfortune in Sweden at the time, for the Swedish king was trying to gain control of the Baltic and he needed warships, but it was a fortunate accident for later generations. The *Vasa* is the world's oldest fully preserved ship of its kind. We can clearly see in its hull the tumble-home curve, which made the ship narrower on its upper decks than at the waterline, allowing the ship to carry the heavy weight of cannon closer to the midline and thereby reducing the hazard of capsizing.

Inspecting the *Vasa,* naval architects

Hull structure of an English man-of-war, late 1600s.

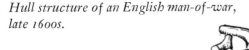

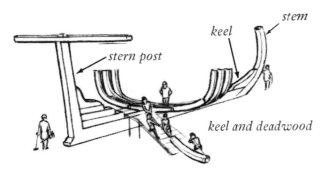

keel and deadwood

stern post

keel

stem

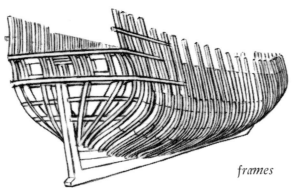

frames

plank

have discovered a good deal about how ships were built at that time. Its timbers are fairly complete and its sternpost is in place. The sternpost had to be strong enough to bear the strain of the rudder. In order to stand this strain, it could not be pieced together, as frames and other large pieces were, but had to be made from one solid piece of wood. To fashion a single oak timber forty feet long and sometimes as thick as twenty-eight inches required a really gigantic tree. It was the size of the sternpost (limited by the trees that were available) that limited the size of wooden ships, as much as the fact that wooden hulls were elastic. The longer the hull, the harder it was to make it strong enough to prevent hogging. (*Hogging* means to arch upward in the middle like the back of a hog. In a ship the center tends to arch upward as the result of strains, and the ends droop.)

Other parts of the ship called for other exceptional pieces of wood. The pieces used for the great knee at the prow and those supporting deck beams on gundecks had to be fashioned from trees bent naturally in that approximate shape. These were hard to find because age alone could produce the large trees needed, and it was more profitable to cut trees for timber when they were young. Masts were another problem. Tall, straight trees were cut for board and plank before they reached the towering height required for masts. For the English, New England became a source of supply for such essential timbers. An Englishman writing in 1666 declared: "There is also the very good news of four New England ships with masts for the King; which is a blessing mighty unexpected, and without which, if for nothing else, we must have failed the next year." He meant that their ships could not be put into service without the American masts. A record kept of two great masts sent from Maine in 1650 gives their measurements as 101¼ and 100 feet in length, and crosswise at the butt, 36½ and 38 inches. Very tall timber.

To get such timber was a continual struggle for most countries. The Swedish king could afford to say: "Building small ships is only a waste of young trees." Sweden had enough timber to build many fleets. The Dutch and English were not so fortunate. The Dutch imported Baltic lumber and built thousands of swift smaller ships with it. England shared this Baltic supply until her source was cut off during the many years the country was at war with the Dutch and French. Getting the lumber to build her ships was a serious problem for England, for there were not many trees left in that small country. Laws were passed, and strictly enforced, about the cutting of trees. Compounding the problem was the fact that the English seemed always to be impressed with sheer bigness. Her kings and merchants wanted shipwrights to build the largest possible ships, with the greatest possible number of guns. Had not the size of wooden ships been limited, because of hogging and the size of the sternpost, the world might have seen gargantuan vessels issue from English ports long before the modern English *"Queens."*

The problems of timber did not end with getting it and building it into ships. Two dangerous enemies were the marine borer and dry rot. Whole fleets of ships were put out of action in the 1600s because of dry rot, a condition caused by a fungus growth

broad axe

adz and plane

iron bands

Hewing spar from a single timber.

that reduces wood to powder. The only evidence of the insidious rot is a mushroom-like growth on the outside of the wood. The timbers still look strong, but inside, the creeping white fingers of fungus have destroyed the wood's fiber. Large sections of infected deck and hull would give way at a touch. The warm, moist darkness of the ship's hold was an excellent environment for the fungus. The only way to be rid of it was to replace the wood. Ventilating the ships, a practice that became common in the 1700s, helped somewhat, but when timbers were not fully cured or were floated on rivers to shipyards, the wood was particularly susceptible to the fungus.

The shipworm, or marine borer, is a tiny mollusk—a relative of the snail and the oyster—that flourishes in temperate and warmer waters. A minute shell attached to the ship's hull provides a covering for the animal, which eats away the wood. Once northern ships began sailing in tropic waters, as they did increasingly in the 1600s, the marine borer became a serious problem. Arsenic and many other such compounds were used in mixtures to coat the hulls of ships to prevent the shipworm from attacking, but they were rarely effective. Lead sheets were also tried, but a new problem arose when in the 1600s iron fittings came into common use. The chemical action between the two metals was so destructive that parts of the rudder were sometimes eaten away. The sheathing of ships with copper became practical in the latter part of the 1700s because steam-powered rolling mills could easily produce the thin sheets of that metal. Copper did keep the shipworm out of the hull, but the high cost of this material and the necessity of constant

replacement put an end to the practice.

Guns aboard ship in the 1600s and after also presented a number of problems. Warships came in all sizes; some had single gun decks, while others had two full gun decks, plus guns on the main deck. There were also guns in the stern. Smaller ones were used on the stern decks and bow. Cast-iron guns became the principal artillery afloat in the 1700s, although the more expensive bronze ship's guns were always preferred. Cast bronze was tougher than iron, and less metal was needed in bronze guns. Thus, although bronze is much heavier than iron, the bronze pieces were usually lighter. Another advantage of bronze was that, unlike iron, it did not rust. And it could be recast when the gun wore out, whereas the iron piece had to be sold as scrap when its use as artillery was exhausted.

The guns used aboard ship in the 1600s were hollow-cast; that is, the melted metal was poured around a core. When the core was removed the bore was formed. (The bore is the hole in the tube.) A Swiss gunmaker changed all that in 1740 when he cast the gun solid, then drilled the bore. This made it possible to manufacture more uniform big guns. Cast-iron guns were always rough on the outside, although smooth-bored. Bronze cannon could be put in lathes so that the outside could be smoothed, too. The weight of these cast guns was impressive. A cannon capable of shooting a ball weighing thirty-two pounds weighed two tons. (It required eighteen pounds of gunpowder for each shot.) The path of the shot was a "flat" one. To illustrate, a baseball pitcher throws a ball "flat" out, a batter hits a ball up "high" or "curved." The path taken by a missile through the air is called trajectory. The guns aboard ships shot missiles in flat trajectory, and the shot went toward the target in relatively level flight. Firing through small gunports did not allow the guns to be elevated, so flat-trajectory guns were more practical. They were fairly accurate up to about half a mile. A gun in use in 1600 could throw a shot almost as far as a gun of 1850. Solid cast-iron shot, the famous cannonball, was the most common ammunition. At 100-yard range a 24-pound shot would penetrate 4½ feet of solid oak. Taking a fairly accurate aim at the waterline, a gunner might sink or seriously damage a vessel with only a few rounds.

The bigger the ship, the more cannon it could carry. Yet the number of cannon alone did not necessarily make a ship a good man-of-war. The French proved this time and again. French ships with two decks and 72 or 74 guns were easier to handle and could probably fire as many broadsides as the heavier, harder-handling English ships of the same size with three decks and more than 74 guns. The English were always eager to capture French ships so that they could imitate the design. At the same time, Dutch tactics were the best at sea, and the English were quick to adopt them. "Never a borrower be" did not hold for the English. By borrowing the best from her enemies, England had become one of the greatest oceanic powers by the early 1700s.

Although the English imitated the French in shipbuilding, Dutch ships were the models used in most European countries. Peter the Great, czar of Russia, made a personal study of the ships in Holland in 1667. What he saw were light, shallow-draught vessels with little ornamentation.

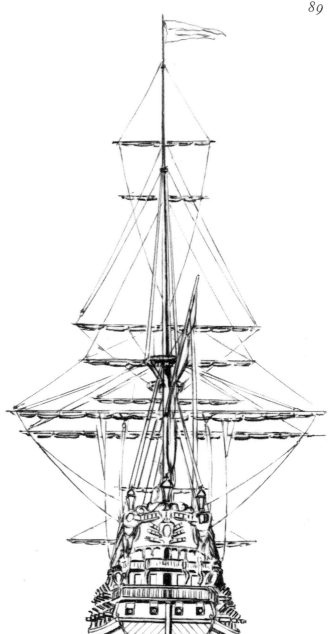

84-gun ship, French, late 1600s.

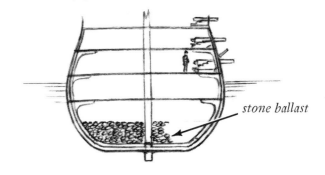

stone ballast

Dutch fluyt, early 1600s.

Dutch galleon, same era.

The beakhead curved gracefully upward. The upper portion of Dutch galleons were clinker-built to make the bulwarks and decks aft stronger. Frenchmen, too, went to Holland to study Dutch ships. The wide, light, flat-sterned hulls the French saw became the basis for the swift sailing ships they later built. The fault with these swift, light galleons was that they were less able than the heavy English ships to withstand broadside firing. English ships sat low in the water with the stern squared off high above the water level. This created a surer platform from which guns could be fired. And while the Dutch and French could, in good weather, fire shot for shot from their two-deckers, the English three-decker could pound away with devastating results so long as the ship's officers kept a sharp eye on the lowest gunports to keep them from flooding.

An English admiral wrote about this condition on ships, saying: "I have now two ships of 90 and 3 or 80 guns that can make use of their lower tiers of guns if it blow a cap full of wind." The implication is that his other ships, which were in the majority, could not use their heaviest guns (32-pounders) if the wind was blowing at all, for opening the ports on the lowest tier would cause these ships to flood.

The Dutch merchant ship called the *fluyt,* or flyboat, was the outstanding trade ship of the 1600s. The fluyt had a round stern and relatively flat bottom and in the earlier days of the century was narrow, with sloping sides. Gradually the deck was widened, and, like the galleon type of merchant ship, the fluyt took on a bulbous look. (No matter what the type of ship, if it was used extensively for bulky cargo, it grew broader.) The Dutch used a minimum of sail on their fluyts: two on the bowsprit, two on the foremast, two on the mainmast —all square—and either a lateen alone on the mizzenmast, or the lateen with a square sail above. Holland could not readily supply the many seamen that her thousands and thousands of ships needed. But by keeping the handling of the ship as simple as possible, a crew of ten could do the work that would ordinarily require a crew three times as large.

Reefing the sail, which had not been done for a long time, was reintroduced. The use of reef points required a sailor to work on the yards more frequently, so with the reef points came the use of the *footrope*, which ran along and below the yard and was used by the sailor when he was aloft.

The *studding sail* was introduced in the last part of the 1600s. Stud sails in rectangular or triangular shape were attached to the end of the yard on an extended spar, increasing the sail area. In addition, triangular sails called staysails were placed between the masts running fore-and-aft. The *jib* was a triangular staysail stretching from the end of the jib-boom on the bowsprit to the fore-topmast head in big ships, and from the bowsprit to the masthead in smaller craft. The jib-boom was simply an extension of the bowsprit. When the jib was first introduced many ships retained their square spritsail and spritsail topsail, but gradually these were given up in favor of the triangular foretop staysail, commonly called the jib.

The adoption of the triangular staysail at the bow took well over a century—a graphic example of how slowly ship rigging changed. Triangular fore-and-aft sails had been used for hundreds of years on small craft. The Dutch carried them at the bows of large ships in the last part of the 1600s, along with two square sails. A jib-boom was added and a jib carried in front of the spritsail topmast, while a second jib was carried behind. In the 1700s the flagpole mast on the bowsprit was no longer in use, and both square sails were carried under the bowsprit, while the jibs were carried above. In the late 1700s the use of square sails at the bow was abandoned on most ships, but some still carried them until well into the 1800s. It was only during the last years of wooden sailing ships that they acquired the look most people now associate with sailing ships, when they carried inner, outer and flying jibs and a fore-topsail staysail. So, from two square sails at the bow in the 1600s, the rigging of the sailing ships grew to four triangular staysails just as the steamship was appearing.

The fireship was often used when attacking enemy shipping, especially in a harbor that could be patrolled to prevent an easy getaway. A fireship could be any ship loaded with combustibles, with the porthole covers hinged at the bottom so they could not close accidentally. The ship was set afire and sent in among the enemy's ships in harbor. Fire was so feared aboard wooden ships that the mere sight of a fireship often caused panic in a crowded harbor. If the operation was successful the enemy ships would be forced either to come out and fight, or stay in the harbor and burn. Many a crew was roused out to douse down decks and rigging or chop away anchors when the alarm was given.

In the late 1600s the French introduced the *bomb ketch,* which they used to destroy

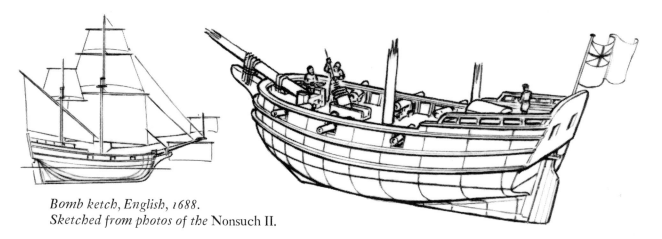

Bomb ketch, English, 1688.
Sketched from photos of the Nonsuch II.

pirate strongholds in North Africa. The bomb ketch was a regular square-rigged ship with the foremast left out. Heavy mortars were carried toward the prow. Mounted on a revolving platform, they could be aimed in any direction. Until the 1800s, heavy stones weighing a hundred pounds or more were used as missiles. In the 1800s two-hundred-pound shells were used. They were put into the mortar's muzzle with block and tackle. French mortars were relatively light, weighing slightly over a thousand pounds; those the English used weighed twice as much.

The construction of the bomb ketch, which was used in the bombardment of towns, had to be extra strong. Its deck beams were massive and heavily reinforced so the ship could withstand the terrific shock of recoil. The rigging of the ship included a square sail on the mainmast and both a lateen and a square topsail on the aftermast. It also carried a square spritsail and a spritsail topsail. Two triangular staysails were attached to the mainmast and bowsprit where the foremast had been. The two-masted ship called a ketch that was developed later was rigged only with fore-and-aft sail, and the mainmast on these

coastal ketches was moved much closer to the bow.

English bomb ships with solid decks and reinforcing studs were used in 1814 during the bombardment of Fort McHenry, the fort defending Baltimore, Maryland. During the twenty-five-hour siege the English fired between 1,500 and 1,800 bombs, rockets, and shells. The enormous exploding bombs caused only moderate damage to the fort, which was built from a French design. When the English withdrew, it was found that one 186-pound bomb had struck the powder magazine, but it had failed to explode. Casualties were low, with only four men killed and twenty-four wounded during the entire bombardment.

All navies began rating their warships in the 1600s. Before this time, sea battles had been free-for-alls without much order. But now ships gave battle in single file along a battle line. Rating, or classifying, ships-of-the-line became the practice. Ships-of-the-line were all supposed to be able to sail at roughly the same speed and carry approximately the same number of guns. Small ships in the line would then not be forced to face the broadsides of much larger ships. A first-rate ship had a hundred guns or more and was usually a three-decker. A second-rate ship carried 90 guns and more. The third-rate ship was usually a two-decker with 74 guns or more. This was the most common ship employed in line fighting. The classifications went as low as sixth-rate. In actual battle the fleet might consist, for example, of one first-rate, two second-rate and seven third-rate ships. On the other hand, the opposing fleet might be made up of twelve third-rate ships and a few smaller ships with 50 or more guns aboard. Ships with fewer than 50 guns were supposedly not included in the battle line, yet when the time for engagement arrived it was sometimes necessary to use them, and even ships of lower rate.

"Line ahead" or file formation provided the best means of using broadside fire, but it had other advantages. There were severe penalties imposed for those who left the line, and this prevented individual attempts to capture and loot injured enemy ships. The penalties and line fighting also tended

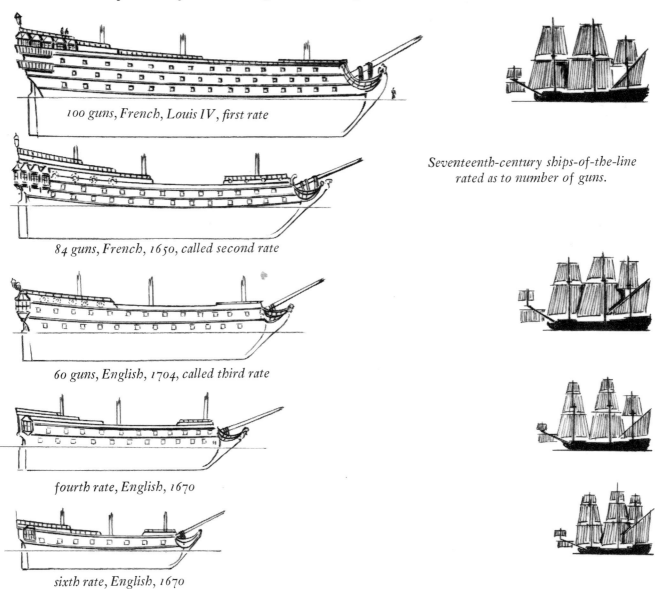

100 guns, French, Louis IV, first rate

84 guns, French, 1650, called second rate

60 guns, English, 1704, called third rate

fourth rate, English, 1670

sixth rate, English, 1670

Seventeenth-century ships-of-the-line rated as to number of guns.

Armed jacht, Dutch, 1620.

Sprit rig with leeboards.

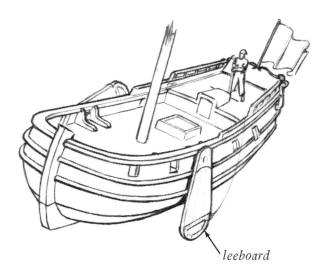

leeboard

to deter ships from deserting during battle. Also, to fight in formation required drilling, which developed better officers and seamen and was good for discipline and order. Earlier seamanship had stressed the glories of individual ship action—the "I'll get mine, you get yours" sort of fighting. With the better coordinated fighting in line order, true navies came into existence and the modern naval traditions of fixed and cooperative tactics began.

The ship-of-the-line was soon put into action in a royal seesawing of wars to gain control of fishing grounds and trade routes. In June 1666 the English fleet was badly beaten by the Dutch in a desperate battle that lasted four days. Twenty English ships were sunk, burned, or captured. During the remainder of June and July the Dutch blockaded the Thames. On July 25 the English fleet, refitted, slipped out to sea and blockaded the Dutch coast, burning 160 Dutch merchantmen. The English king, thinking the Dutch had had enough, laid the fleet up, as was usual during winter. It was a quiet winter, but in the spring the Dutch raided the Thames. The English navy, lying quietly at anchor, was the target. Causing terror and confusion, the Dutch surprised the English and burned, smashed and took ships as they pleased. Now both sides *had* had enough, and peace was declared. However, five years later they were at it again.

A few years afterward a French fleet of 68 line-of-battle ships fought against 33 English warships supplemented in the English line by an added 22 Dutch ships. The English and the Dutch, no longer at war but allies now, were beaten back. The next year the French were defeated by the

Anglo-Dutch fleet. And so it went, on and on, with the French attacking an Anglo-Dutch convoy of 400 ships and sinking 90, and the English and Dutch retaliating. Then, at the very end of the century, the English did something that so surprised the whole of Europe that little else was discussed in naval circles. The English king ordered his large fleet to remain at sea through the winter. It had never been done before, and its success was the beginning of year-round fleet action. And action there was; in England the period from 1697 to 1815 comprised 64 years of war and only 55 years of peace.

Besides the ships-of-the-line, the galleon-like merchantmen and the fluyt, other ships sailed the sea during the 1600s, among them working yachts like the famous little *Half Moon,* a Dutch ship. The word *jacht* meant "swift craft" or "hunter." These yachts were used as fishing ships or for dispatch or scouting work. The working yachts looked somewhat like small fluyts, except they were two-masted. Other craft were given the name "jacht": for example, the single-masted fore-and-aft-rigged pleasure boat. In Holland these small yachts had *leeboards,* large egg-shaped boards placed toward the center at each side. At times, under sail, they were lowered into the water to prevent the ship from drifting. Leeboards were used on small open boats in other countries also.

In 1609 Henry Hudson, an Englishman working for the Dutch, sailed his yacht, the *Half Moon,* into what is now New York harbor. He was looking for the fabled passage to the Orient. It was his third voyage of exploration in North American waters. He investigated the magnificent lower and

Dutch jacht, gaff rig, 1660.

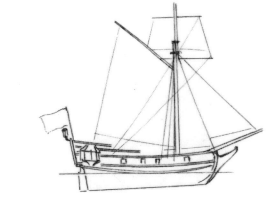

upper bays of New York. When he first sighted the "Great North River" (later named the Hudson), he was certain he had found the mysterious northwest passage. He sailed the *Half Moon* upstream for eleven days, to about where Albany is to-day, before deciding he had made a mistake. When he sailed back to Holland his voyage had given the Dutch a claim in the New World. In 1610 Dutch traders began working in the Hudson Valley. They explored much of the country, including Long Island Sound, the Connecticut River, Cape Cod and the Massachusetts coast. To the south they explored the Delaware River and Bay. In 1614 the New Netherland Company was founded in Holland, and just below Albany the company built Fort Nassau. A trading post was set up on Manhattan Island the same year. By then many trading yachts, in company with larger ships, were regularly crossing the Atlantic between Holland and New York, which soon became the most cosmopolitan of all the colonial cities.

Other well-known ships used in the colonization of the United States were galleonlike three-masted cargo ships and two-masted pinnaces. The 140 settlers of Jamestown, Virginia, sailed from London in December 1606 on three small ships, the *Goodspeed*, the *Susan Constant*, and the pinnace *Discovery*. They reached Chesapeake Bay on April 26, 1607, and in May selected Jamestown as the site for their colony.

No one knows much about the famous *Mayflower*, which brought a shipload of colonists to Massachusetts in 1620. At the time the voyage was not considered important. But the *Mayflower* was probably sim-

Half Moon *standing up the North River, 1609.*
Vessel and rig are guesswork.

Contemporary representation of ship Ark, *1633.*

ilar to the *Ark,* the flat-sterned, galleonlike three-masted ship that brought the young Leonard Calvert, a brother of Lord Baltimore, to Maryland in 1634. Calvert's coming was somewhat different from that of earlier colonists, for among the 200 settlers he brought with him were twenty "gentlemen." The ship that accompanied the *Ark* was the two-masted pinnace *Dove.* In the early 1950s plaster reliefs representing the ship *Ark* and the pinnace *Dove* were uncovered in England. These were ceiling decorations in Hook House, part of the marriage portion of Anne Arundell, who married Cecil Calvert, the second Lord Baltimore. These reliefs are the only known representations of any of the ships used by English settlers in North America which were made at the time the voyages took place.

In the 1600s the voyages of exploration were fewer than in previous centuries, for most of the world had been "discovered" by Europeans. Many attempts were made to find a passage to the East through the polar regions. Henry Hudson's investigation of New York harbor was made during one of his four trips into the Arctic. On one of these voyages two of his men believed they saw a mermaid. "She played for a moment on the surface of the sea and then, with a flurry of her fishy tail, disappeared in the cold depths." On his last voyage in 1611 Hudson, his son and seven others were set adrift in an open boat when the crew mutinied. Weak and ill from wintering in the frozen north, they were lost among the ice packs and never seen again.

The discoveries of a Dutchman, Abel Janszoon Tasman, in the 1600s did a great deal to broaden European geographical knowledge. Tasman was searching for a

Contemporary representation of pinnace Dove, *1633.*

fabulously rich continent believed to exist in the southern Pacific. This continent was first reported by Marco Polo in the thirteenth century. What Tasman discovered was quite different. He sailed with a fluyt and a yacht in 1642 and explored large parts of the coasts of Tasmania, New Zealand, Tonga, Fiji and other islands. He circumnavigated the continent of Australia, and the charts which he drew were so exact that they could be used today. The renowned Captain Cook used Tasman's information on his voyage in the Pacific in 1770.

Tasman's story is a wonderful one to come upon because his was so different from previous voyages of discovery. He worked in a quiet, professional manner. Having been sent out by the Dutch East India Company to find gold, silver and jewels,

Tasman himself seemed genuinely interested in charting new places. He was excited by the sight of a previously unknown bay. The rocks, the water, the trees, the people he met all came alive in his reports. It was as if he were saying: "It would be fine to find gold and silver, but look at what's actually here. See, the northern coast of Australia is not part of New Guinea as you thought."

But the managers of the East India Company were not impressed. Government officials in Holland were not moved, either. There was no bloody drama, no roaring thunder of guns, no ship returning with stolen fortunes—all of which they had come to expect from ventures such as Tasman's. Yet, when the reports are read, it is impossible not to come away with the feeling that Tasman was satisfied with his work. He knew he had done a good job, and so do we.

Without a doubt Tasman and his fellow Dutchmen were the most extraordinary seamen of the 1600s. Holland had twice as many ships as France, England and Germany combined. Hers were swift and sturdy and their crews healthy. Ever since 1593 all Dutch ships had carried sauerkraut aboard to combat scurvy, and vegetable patches were often cultivated on the ships. Even before 1593 the Dutch had discovered that oranges were successful in treating the disease. Not satisfied with these precautions, the Dutch created settlements in such places as Capetown and St. Helena for the specific purpose of keeping ships supplied with fresh food for Dutch seamen.

The English, French and others could have profited by following the Dutch example, but since they failed to do so, thousands of men died. An English admiral judged that ten thousand English seamen died of scurvy within a twenty-year period. Beginning with 1600 the English East India Company did supply their ships with oranges, but the Royal Navy did not follow this example, and men in the Navy continued to die. It was not until 1794 that citrus fruit juice became part of the Royal Navy sailor's daily rations. They were given the juice of lemons from Malta and Sicily, which were called limes at that time. When the lemons became difficult to obtain the English navy began using the limes from the West Indies, and scurvy broke out again. It was found that limes actually contain very little of the vitamin needed to fight the disease.

The size and design of the larger ships did not change radically during the 1600s.

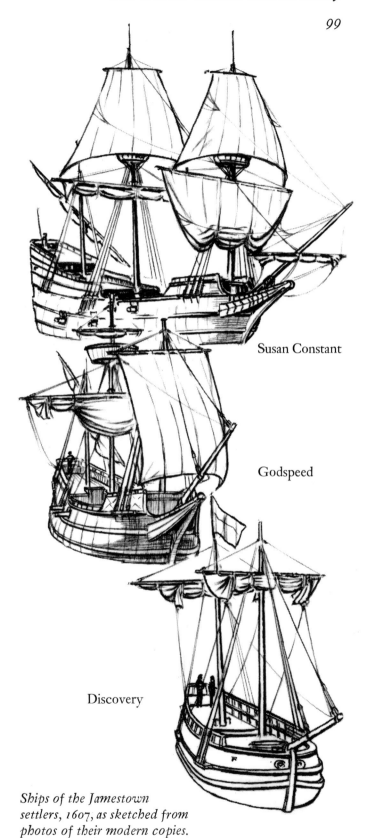

Susan Constant

Godspeed

Discovery

Ships of the Jamestown settlers, 1607, as sketched from photos of their modern copies.

100 But many more ships were sailing the oceans of the world than ever before, and national navies were becoming truly gigantic. Recruiting crews to work in these ships became a serious problem. Holland, being a great power but a small country, hired all the seamen she could get from other countries. In England fishing and trade were encouraged, and crews were not so hard to come by in her many seaports. To make certain that seamen would be available for naval duty in times of emergency, laws were passed restricting the number of foreigners aboard merchant ships, which in effect were used as training ships for the navy. However, living conditions in naval vessels were so grim that the government had to resort to impressment (arrest and detention) to get men to work under these conditions. Often men returning from a voyage of two or three years were seized aboard merchantmen as they sailed into English waters. An ordinary seaman, Edward Coxere, writing about his life, gives a clear picture of conditions in England in the mid-1600s. "Now, being at home again, instead of taking some pleasure with my friends, I was still terrified with the press, for I could not walk the streets without danger, nor sleep in safety." It was not until 1835 that an Act of Parliament ruled that no man could be detained in naval service against his will *for more than five years*. To this day the system of impressment has not been abolished by an Act of Parliament, although, of course, it is no longer in use.

In France, beginning in 1673, impressment in wartime was replaced by conscription, the compulsory enlistment of men for naval service. This system was not popular among either shipowners or sailors, and later in French history it caused a good deal of difficulty for French governments. Conscription worked in a complicated fashion. Depending on the number of seamen working on commercial ships in a particular area, a given number of men were called every few years to serve aboard naval ships. If there were many commercial seamen in a particular area, it meant that many men could be spared for naval duty without injury to commercial shipping. A man registered and was called on to serve one year out of every four. But where fewer commercial seamen were available, great injury to commercial shipping would result if these men were forced to serve in the navy; therefore, in less populated areas commercial seamen would serve for only limited terms. Some served only one out of every five years, others only one year out of every ten. Each year of service was supposed to be divided into two parts, half on duty at full pay and half off at half pay. More often than not a seaman forced to serve in the navy received no pay at all, and he and his family suffered. As a result, a seaman did his best to escape conscription, which eventually led to the depopulation of the French coast. In long wars impressment was still necessary.

Besides the larger seagoing warships and merchant ships for which men were either "pressed" or conscripted, there were many different types of smaller vessels for seamen to work on in the 1600s. In the northern colonies of the North American east coast, shallops, barks, and ketches were most often used, along with small and large pinnaces employed in coastal trading and also often used to carry colonists as well as car-

Ship's longboat, British, about 1730, after H.I. Chapelle.

American 2-mast boat, 1760, after H.I. Chapelle.

Shallops.

Mayflower II's shallop, *as sketched from photos.*

English ketch sketched from a drawing of Newcastle-on-Tyne dated 1724.

English brigantine sketched from a view of Philadelphia dated 1754.

Either vessel might variously have been described as a bark.

goes across the ocean. The *shallop,* used for fishing and some coastal trading, was a double-ended craft using both sails and oars. Sometimes this open double-ended workboat carried a single mast and fore-and-aft sail, and sometimes two masts with square sail.

Barks were simple single-decked vessels with a round stern; usually they were two-masted with square sail. Sometimes a small lateen mizzen was added on the larger barks. The *ketch* was a strongly built fishing vessel. The sails varied from simple fore-and-aft to square. The ketch was generally built small, about 12 tons upward, but there were large oceangoing ketches, too, which carried deep and narrow square sail.

In general, shipbuilding in the United States began with the building of shallops. Larger vessels coming to the colonies at first carried smaller ones to be used once the ships arrived. The *Mayflower* carried a long boat and a shallop, the *Ark* a shallop and a barge. For fishing, the colonists often used Indian dugouts, one of the most ancient types of boats, and in time they became proficient at making them themselves. On Chesapeake Bay this resulted in some incredibly beautiful log canoes. Each canoe was made of one log at first; later, three to five logs were combined to fashion one of the most interesting of all small American sailing craft, the racing Chesapeake Log Canoe.

The details connected with the building of a ship of about 40 tons burden give a revealing insight into French exploration and trading in the North American interior. (The amount of cargo the ship could carry, or its burden, was 40 tons. The average tonnage of a large ship in the 1600s was 250 tons.) LaSalle, the French explorer, had his men fell spruce and oak for this ship above Niagara Falls. A master carpenter directed the building, which began in the snow-covered forest in January 1679. In the spring the vessel was launched with cannon fire and singing and was then towed out into the Niagara River. The builders, swinging their hammocks under the deck, slept in peace out of reach of Indian tomahawks. The ship was named the *Griffin,* and it sailed the Great Lakes. A few months after it was launched, the *Griffin* sank during a severe storm on Lake Huron. Archeologists have discovered and identified its remains near Manitoulin Island. Dated fittings, and a near-giant skeleton that is thought to be that of the pilot, Lucas, have

convinced the finders of its authenticity.

During the 1600s the idea of building a steamboat was first advanced. In 1690 Denis Papin, a French physicist, built the earliest working cylinder-and-piston apparatus using steam. This was merely a mechanical device; it was not used to operate a vehicle, although Papin suggested that it could be used to propel boats. Experiments with steam led to the development of the steam engine during the next century, and when this happened the steamship became a real possibility. It was to be a great step forward, for ships propelled by mechanical means could voyage in all kinds of weather and no matter from which quarter the wind blew, people and goods could be transported with some certainty of schedule.

Pinnace, French, 1670.

Construction of the Griffon, *Niagara River, 1679. Scene and vessel are guesswork.*

HMS Victory, *1805.*
First-rate ship-of-the-line.
Boat in foreground is a barge.

9.
The Last Years:
The 1700s and After

THE LARGEST fighting ships during the last years of sail differed very little from the fighting ships-of-the-line used in the early 1700s. Until the building of iron merchantmen in the mid-1800s, the first-rate wooden battleship was one of the largest types of ship afloat. The ship-of-the-line was really a floating city. Hundreds of men swarmed inside her, tons of supplies filled her hold, and guns jutted from every part of her hull. To build a ship of such immensity usually took five years from the laying of the keel to her launching. The English ship *Victory,* which carried over eight hundred men, was begun in 1759 and launched in 1765 but did not begin to see action until her commissioning in 1778. Her overall length was 328 feet and her gun deck measured 186 feet. To give some idea of the incredible sail area on a first-rate such as the *Victory,* imagine yourself standing on the main deck, which is 40 feet wide. Beyond the deck the sails, when the studsails are added, reach out over the water 78½ feet on each side—a total of 197 feet of sail. Such a ship with

sails billowing must have been a thrilling sight—or, to the enemy, a frightening one.

The *Victory* can be seen at Portsmouth, England, today with stripes of yellow and black on her hull just as Admiral Horatio Nelson instructed all naval ships to be painted. It was on the *Victory* that Nelson was wounded and died during the battle of Trafalgar in 1805. The battle of Cape Trafalgar in the Mediterranean was the final triumph of English naval warfare under sail. This battle took place in the closing years of almost continual competition and war between England and France, a battle for power that had gone on for over a hundred years.

The struggle was an uneven one at sea, for England's navy was twice the size of France's, and England had many more seamen (according to estimates at the time, from six to ten times as many) and many more merchant ships. The English strategy was one of battle and blockade, and it was successful. The French, knowing their navy was not so large as the English, did not seek out the enemy fleet, but rather aimed at raids on English commerce, but were unable to inflict any decisive blow.

All during the 1700s the English and French fought in the West Indies, India, North America and Africa. It was a worldwide war, and a deciding factor in the victory was English shipping. But even more important were the English seamen.

The seaman's life was brutal. He was a prisoner of his ship in times of war. In one period of seven years (1756–1763), 1,512 English seamen were killed in battle and another 133,708 died of disease or were missing. Despite all this, the English spirit overcame such hardships, and English seamen proved good sailors. One of the reasons was that English naval officers were virtually raised at sea, beginning life aboard ship at fifteen during the 1700s, while French officers rarely went to sea. English gunners, too, had an advantage. They were recklessly brave in broadside action, and their guns were better, more effective instruments of destruction. The French, on the other hand, preferred to do their fighting from a distance, attempting to incapacitate the enemy ship by destroying its rigging. French ships were lighter and swifter, but because of their lightness they were more vulnerable to heavy pounding in close fighting.

The French navy, which had been so full of promise during the 1600s, did not develop as expected during the 1700s, partly because the French government was preoccupied with entanglements on land, and because the French seamen hated the system of conscription which caused many men to leave seacoast areas and settle inland. Eventually the French government had to find sailors in Genoa, Nice and other Mediterranean ports, and when these seamen were not available, French peasants, who did not make good sailors, were impressed to serve on the ships. On the other hand, in 1778 the English were able to expand their navy from 16,000 to 60,000 and still keep their merchant ships going. They could do this because the laws forbidding foreigners to work in merchant ships were suspended in times of emergency. These foreign seamen were employed in the commercial fleets of England, while the French used alien seamen aboard their naval vessels. The difference was slight but important, for ill-trained French officers in charge

Gun deck, mid-1700s.

of foreign seamen during battle more than had their hands full. Oddly enough, considering conditions in English ships, the English officers usually had the complete loyalty of their crews.

With the adverse effects of conscription and their evasive battle tactics, it was no wonder the French lost at sea. Besides, England's naval accomplishments during this period are impressive. The records show that from the late 1600s to the middle of the 1800s, England's losses in ships of over 50 guns ran to 26. The losses by her enemies were 336 ships of over 50 guns. A total of 178 of these ships were French—48 of them having been destroyed during operations. Still, the power of the English navy lay in the quality of her seamen and the quantity of her ships. A sober insight into English naval warfare was given by English Admiral Lord Anson in 1744. Lord Anson had been in almost every action and skirmish since 1718, and yet he wrote that he had never seen or heard of an English ship,

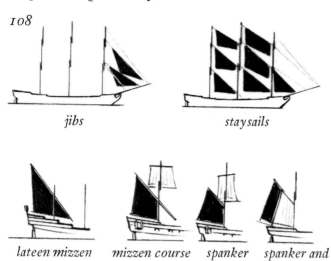

jibs

staysails

lateen mizzen

mizzen course
and square topsail

spanker

spanker and
driver

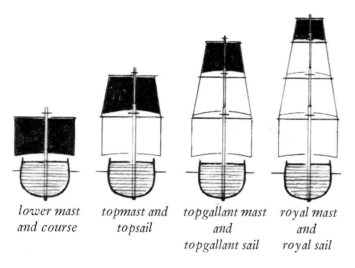

lower mast
and course

topmast and
topsail

topgallant mast
and
topgallant sail

royal mast
and
royal sail

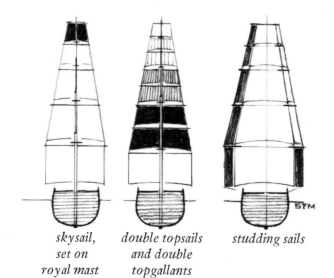

skysail,
set on
royal mast

double topsails
and double
topgallants

studding sails

alone and singly opposed to one of the enemy's of equal force, taking the enemy.

English first- and second-rate ships were similar except for size and number of guns. There were not many of either rate in use at any one time. They seldom left home waters, even in wartime, and they seldom left European waters at all. On these and other ships of over 50 guns the basic square-sail plan was used which had been used in the 1600s. More staysails between the fore and main and between the main- and miz-zenmasts came into use slowly. The only really new features about these later ships were the improvement of the hull to make it more seaworthy and the introduction of a new mizzen sail. The top of the lateen sail was cut off, and the spanker sail was the result. Another sail, the driver, was set above the spanker. For a while the two sails remained separate, but by the end of the 1700s they were joined into one large sail.

Another sail, a square one called the royal, was added above the topgallant on larger ships during the 1700s. In warships it was always set flying, that is, hoisted into position, from the deck, and when furled, it was taken down on deck. In mer-chant ships the royal became a part of the standing sail, with the royal yard left aloft.

The masts from which these sails hung were becoming difficult to obtain, for rea-sons discussed earlier, so "made masts," or "built-up masts" were used. These were made from great pieces of wood cut like wedges of cheese, eight of them fitted to-gether and bound at first with rope and in later years with iron hoops. These built-up masts were divided into stages. The stoutest carried the yard for the mainsail; capping that mast was a slighter one which carried the topsail, and so on. These masts were footed into enormous blocks on the floor above the keel (the mizzenmast was sometimes set into the orlop deck) and kept in place by a complicated arrangement of stays and backstays, trusses, ties, caps, crosstrees, braces and wedges.

The *frigate* became an important part of all navies in the 1700s. During the preceding century a small, fast vessel, also called a frigate, with six to twelve guns had been in use. At the beginning of this century the frigate carried 24 to 28 guns and a crew of about 160. Its main features during the early 1700s were a clean line from stem to stern with no outstanding structures, and guns mounted on a single flush deck. A flush deck runs from stem to stern without interruption. At the end of the century, frigates were generally armed with from 24 to 44 guns mounted on a single flush gun deck and on both forecastle and half-deck, which were connected by gangways along the side of the ship. After 1815 the gangways also carried guns, and such frigates looked as if they had two complete decks. They were called "double-banked frigates."

The frigates of the United States were often so fast that European seamen did not believe them to be frigates at all, but some other type of ship. Two of these U.S. frigates are still afloat. The oldest surviving ship of the United States fleet, the *Constellation*, can be boarded today in the harbor of Baltimore, Maryland. The *Constellation* was launched at Baltimore on September 7, 1797, and was ready for her shakedown cruise in June of 1798. It was during this cruise that the *Constellation* defeated the French frigate *L'Insurgente* in the Carib-

American frigate of 1797.

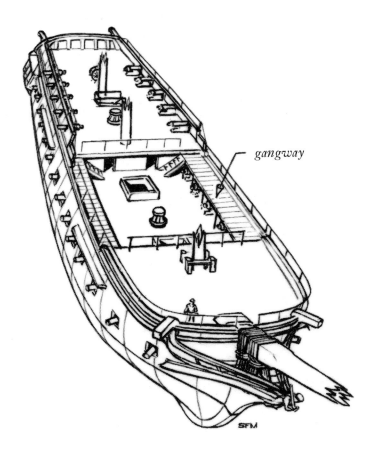

gangway

bean in February 1799. She was the first ship of the Federal Navy to defeat an opponent in sea battle. Along on that cruise was another U.S. frigate, the *Constitution*, which had been launched at Boston, Massachusetts, on October 21, 1797, or about two months after the *Constellation*. The *Constitution* is also still afloat today.

The history of the *Constellation* is a long one. She fought in the Mediterranean at Tripoli in 1802, then in U.S. waters, then off Peru in the Pacific. She was the first U.S. ship to penetrate Chinese inland waters. Serving as the flagship of the U.S. fleet in African waters during the Civil War (1861-1865), the *Constellation* captured three slave ships and freed almost a thousand slaves. In 1880 when Ireland suffered a famine she carried food there. In 1940, just before the United States entered the Second World War, President Roosevelt made the *Constellation* the flagship of the Atlantic fleet.

The hull of the frigate *Constellation* is 203 feet long; her overall length is about 260 feet. When she was cruising the Caribbean in 1799 she had a crew of 313, which included marines. She carried 38 guns, mostly 24-pounders. The gunports of the *Constellation* were set high in her hull, about eight feet above water level. This meant that she and other U.S. frigates built along the same lines could be sailed hard in rough seas. She was called "The Yankee Race Horse," and since the Federal Navy was such a small one and faced such enormous odds, the *Constellation* and other American frigates had one distinct advantage: if they could not defeat the enemy, they could outrun them. The *Constellation* was overhauled many times. Several of her

nails are stamped 1797, 1808, or 1812. In 1829 her original flat transom stern was removed and replaced with a round one. In 1853 she was lengthened by 11½ feet. At that time she carried only 22 guns.

The U.S. frigates were longer and broader than European frigates. They carried royals as well as a gaff topsail above the spanker. They also carried a fore-and-aft sail beyond the spanker called a *ringtail sail*. Such ships cost a lot of money, and although the U.S. was very young and very poor, her builders were instructed to use the very best materials that could possibly be obtained. So even though the ships were few, they were the best.

Besides the improvement in naval vessels, merchant ships during the 1700s underwent many changes. The English did some experimenting, but the majority of research in hull design was done in France. Up until this time the bow had been considered all-important. The attitude of shipbuilders was that the rest of the hull could take care of itself. Abbé Bossuet showed how the movement of water around the rudder could make steering easier. Shipbuilders thought his ideas odd, so they did not change the shape of their ships. Then another Frenchman, M. Romme, began conducting experiments with ship models in water, a system still in use today. Gradually the shape of the hull was changed to allow the water to flow past the bow, around the midsection of the hull, and in toward the rudder.

The large merchantmen of the late 1700s and early 1800s were built along these lines. They traveled to the East and West Indies from Europe and were really armed transports, some carrying as many as 54 guns.

38-gun frigate Constellation, *1797-1853.*

163'

176'

Hull drawings based on drafts by H.I. Chapelle.

Constellation *as rebuilt into a spar-decked corvette, 1853–1854. Still afloat.*

SFM

Bounty, *1787,*
as sketched from photos of Lunenburg-built Bounty II.

They were many-decked, roomy ships with three masts, square-rigged with fore-and-aft sails added. They traveled in convoy, with crews aboard going through drills and gunnery practice as in the navy. Some compared in size with third- and fourth-rate naval vessels.

Nearly everyone is familiar with the English ship *Bounty,* a small armed merchant ship of the 1700s. The mutiny aboard the *Bounty* has set many writers' minds to work, and book after book has been written about Captain Bligh and his acting mate Fletcher Christian. The *Bounty's* overall length was 100 feet; at the waterline it was 84 feet 6 inches, and its keel measured 69 feet 9 inches. It was fitted with four four-pounders and ten swivel guns, and was square-rigged, carrying royals; the fore-and-aft sails included jibs and spanker.

The *Bounty* had been sent out in 1787 to gather breadfruit trees in the Pacific for transplanting in the English colonies of the West Indies. Breadfruit was thought to be a good source of food for the slaves work-

ing the English plantations. Captain Bligh sailed to Tahiti. He spent five months there loading his ship with live trees. Christian, along with other members of the crew, found life in the Pacific too good to leave, and on the return voyage he seized Bligh and forced him into the *Bounty's* launch. Eighteen officers and men went with Bligh. The ship's launch was small, only 23 feet long. With the men, water, a little pork and bread it was overloaded, and the gunwale came within seven inches of the water.

On the morning of April 28, 1789, the world's most famous open boat voyage began. With compass and quadrant Captain Bligh navigated over 3,000 miles of ocean. For forty-one days he and his men fought the sun, the ocean, starvation and thirst. The captain went on to a distinguished career. Fletcher Christian and some of the mutinous crew, accompanied by a few Tahitians, took the *Bounty* to Pitcairn Island, where they settled. It was not long before they were at each other's throats, and the little island became a place of treachery and murder.

Another merchant ship common on all oceans during the 1700s and 1800s was the *whale ship*. Whale oil and bone were important products, and fleets of whale ships covered the Atlantic and Pacific. The Dutch had sent out 1,652 whaling ships between 1699 and 1708. They used fluyts as parent ships for the sturdy whale boats. Later a ship that was stubby at both ends was used in European whaling. Called a *bootschip,* it had a heavy timber built across the stern to support the open boats used to hunt the whales. With a fat, flat rounded stem and stern and looking like a floating loaf of bread (square-ended), it became the model for whalers. These broad-beamed ships were called "blubber wagons" and "spouters." Sailors joked that they were built by the mile and cut off in lengths. Whalers were also called "stove-boats" because amidships they carried large brick structures which housed the furnace, and boilers used for boiling oil out of the whale blubber. Heavy cranes hung from their bulwarks carried the open boats in which the men chased the whales.

There was no romance in whaling. A whaling ship went out and stayed out until she was loaded with oil and bone. This might take three or four years, even five.

Bootschip with whale.

*American sloop,
1841, after Chapelle.*

*Chebacco boat, 1800,
successor to the colonial
shallop. Early form of
New England fishing
schooner.*

*Grand Banks halibut schooner,
about 1840.*

*Grand Banks
fishing schooner,
about 1900.*

The chase, harpooning and lancing of the whale was a dangerous business, often ending in death or serious injury. Stripping and loading the blubber aboard ship so that the oil could be boiled out was an unpleasantly smelly and fatiguing job. Whaling was a dangerous business for ships as well as men. In one year alone, 33 ships were crushed by Arctic ice.

The *sloop* was the most common ship in the North American colonies in the early 1700s. The first sloops were double-ended, with round sterns and a single mast with fore-and-aft sail. Later the stern was squared, and sometimes square main and topsails were added. The sloop in colonial waters developed from European models. Used for trade, it fell into the large-small class of craft.

One sloop that gained a measure of fame was the *Swallow*, a sixth-rate sloop of 14 guns that had seen service in the English navy. The Englishman Philip Carteret sailed the *Swallow* around the world from 1766 to 1769. He was searching for the elusive southern continent that so many men thought existed in the Pacific. His trip was something of a disaster. The *Swallow* leaked and rolled and was buffeted around the oceans. It was not a good ship. It had been outfitted in haste. The year before Carteret sailed, the English government had sent ships to look for another vague continent in the southern Atlantic. Then they heard that the French had established a settlement in South America for the express purpose of finding the Pacific continent. Jealous of French overseas development, the English could not bear the thought of the new French threat. That was the mood in which Carteret was shipped out on his unhappy voyage. Nevertheless, he did give the English a good glimpse of the Orient and whet the appetite of the businessmen back home for development of commerce with China.

Another common type of vessel built during the last years of the sailing ship was the *schooner*. Although tradition in the U.S. claims that the first schooner built was constructed in Gloucester, Massachusetts, in 1713, schooners actually were used in Holland in the 1600s. The early schooner was a two-masted vessel, mainly rigged with fore-and-aft sail. Sometimes square topsails were added to both masts, and a square sail on the foremast. Schooners had sharp bows and square sterns. In later years schooners were built with as many as seven masts.

Brigs, brigantines and snows were also in common use for coastal and foreign trade in Europe and America during the 1700s and 1800s. All were two-masted ships with square sails on the foremast. They all carried jibs, and in the early days some carried spritsails below the bowsprit. A *brigantine* carried a fore-and-aft sail on her mainmast. The *brig* carried square sails on her mainmast, plus a fore-and-aft gaffsail, the brigsail. On the *snow* the brigsail was carried on a spar capped onto the lower part of the mainmast just behind the mast. This, in effect, gave the brigsail a mast of its own on the snow. The square sails on those ships were long and narrow, and the use of studding sails was common. They all carried staysails between the fore and mainmasts.

One of the most interesting scientific voyages ever made took place in the 1830s on an English ten-gun brig. The brig's

brig

brigantine

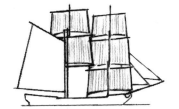

snow

hermaphrodite brig

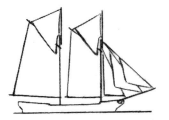

schooner

topsail schooner

116 name was *Beagle,* and aboard her sailed a remarkable young man, twenty-two-year-old Charles Darwin. The *Beagle* was on a surveying cruise to South America, and Darwin was the ship's naturalist. Nothing escaped this young man's keen eyes. During the voyage he developed a theory of how coral atolls and reefs were formed, and years later he was proved right. He had wonderfully exciting adventures traveling in the wild pampas and through jungles; collecting fossils, plants, and animals; and taking notes about musical frogs and phosphorescent insects and about how grasses grew. Darwin kept a detailed journal that was later published as *The Voyage of the Beagle.* In it stories of Indian attacks, storms at sea, riding and climbing in the Andes are interwoven with the most exact and unusual scientific observations.

The captain of the *Beagle,* Robert Fitz Roy, only four years older than Darwin, was also a remarkable man. His job was to survey the shores of Chile, Peru, and some of the Pacific islands, and to carry a chain of chronometrical measurements around the world. Invented by John Harrison, an Englishman, the chronometer is an instrument

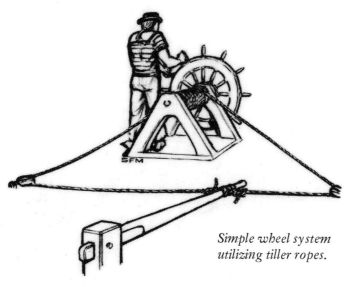

Simple wheel system utilizing tiller ropes.

for measuring time. It is *not* just a big wristwatch but a much more complicated timepiece, with special balances and other features that make it invaluable for use at sea. Judging longitude is a very simple calculation if you have an instrument that will tell you accurately, through gale and hail, what time it is at the Royal Observatory in Greenwich, England—the location of the zero longitude meridian. Noting the time of the sun's highest ascent on the chronometer kept at Greenwich time, you figure that local noon will be one hour earlier or later for every 15 degrees of longitude east or west of Greenwich. Judging longitude with a ship's chronometer running just 15 seconds fast will cause an error of many miles.

Another help in navigation during the 1700s was the introduction of the steering wheel in the early part of the century. Ropes ran from the big double wheel through pulleys to the tiller, which manipulated the rudder. Venice officially adopted the wheel in 1719. But the whipstaff, the wheel's predecessor, was still common in ships into the 1800s. The literature and history of the American colonies along the Atlantic coast contain many more references to the whipstaff than to the wheel.

The Baltimore Clipper was a popular ship in the North American colonies during the Revolutionary War (1776-1783) and later. By the early 1800s it was being used by smugglers, pirates, and slavers who needed a fast vessel for their illegal activities. It was a long, light ship with very little rigging and could be handled by a small crew. It had extremely rakish masts; that is, the masts inclined fifteen or more degrees from perpendicular, as if falling backward. There was also a great rake to stem and sternposts. Its wide, clear decks were flush. The speed and success of the larger, heavier armed Baltimore Clippers attracted European designers, who copied the type. Although fast, the ships could not carry much cargo, and consequently did not make much money for their owners in legal trade. Gradually they were used only for smuggling slaves and as pirate ships in the West Indies. These ships became associated with lawless activities to such a degree that they were hunted, captured or destroyed whenever possible. By the 1830s the type had vanished altogether.

In the 1830s and '40s American shipbuilders began building "clipper ships." (They sailed at a good "clip.") Their design was different from the earlier Baltimore Clipper. The clipper ship *Great Republic*, launched in 1853, was the largest wooden vessel ever built. It was 325 feet long and 53 feet wide. At it was about to begin its first voyage a fire broke out aboard. The damage was repaired, but the hull and rig were cut down, so no one knows how the original ship would have sailed.

One of the most famous clippers, the *Cutty Sark*, is still in existence in England. It was built in 1869 to bring from China tea, a high-profit cargo that did not require so much space (dollar profit per pound) as cheaper and bulkier items. The sleek clipper ship provided excellent transport in such cases. These later clipper ships were often built with iron frames, but with wooden keels and planking. Many other parts, such as chains, pulleys and mast caps, were also made of iron. The *Cutty Sark,* like most clippers, is a three-masted ship. (The *Great Republic* originally had

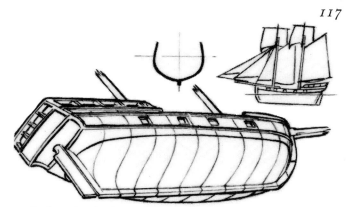

Full-ended hull of New England schooner, about 1750.

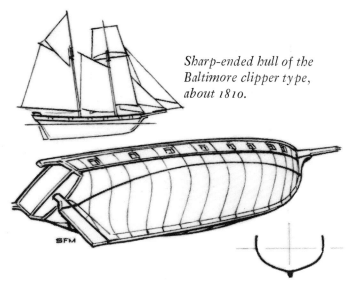

Sharp-ended hull of the Baltimore clipper type, about 1810.

four masts.) It carried square sail on all three masts, plus a number of fore-and-aft sail. The large topsail was very difficult to handle, especially during rough weather, and in 1841 Captain Robert Forbes, an American, introduced the double topsail to replace it. Thereafter two sails took the place of the previous single topsail: the upper topsail and the lower topsail. Later a double topgallant was also used. Skysails, the sail above the royal, were sometimes added, and above the skysail another sail, the moonraker. American cap-

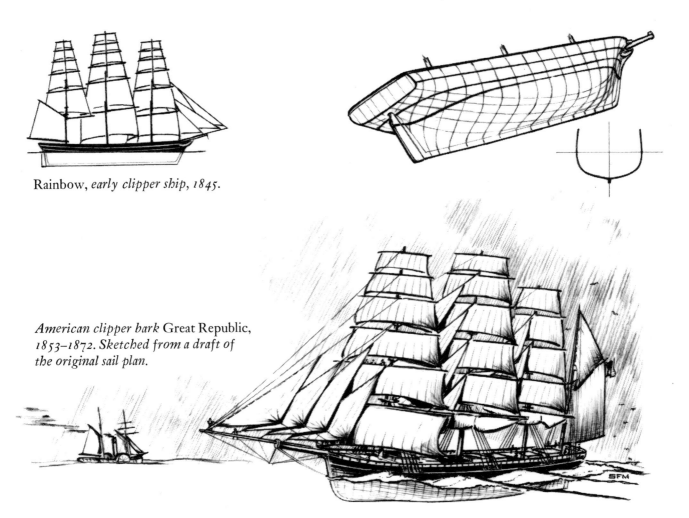

Rainbow, *early clipper ship, 1845.*

American clipper bark Great Republic, *1853–1872. Sketched from a draft of the original sail plan.*

tains seemed particularly fond of these sails, especially the skysail. Clipper ships raced from New York to San Francisco in less than a hundred days, but when railroad tracks stretched from the Atlantic to the Pacific the clipper ship's use was somewhat curtailed on this route.

Even before the extreme clipper ships were built it was discovered that iron plate could be used for the hulls of sailing vessels. Not only was the iron plate durable; it reduced the hazard of fire. Later, even masts, yards, and spars were made of steel tubing. Hemp lines gave way to steel wires. But by this time, after a period of experimentation with ships using both sail and steam, the steamship had come into its own. By 1870 engine-powered battleships made of metal were carrying guns weighing as much as thirty-eight tons each. Steel plating was first used by the English, who built seven steel battleships in 1892. They were 380 feet long and 75 feet wide and carried heavy artillery that made the cannon used on wooden sailing ships look quaint. "Full speed ahead!" became the battle cry, and with smoke pouring from their funnels, the deafening noise from their guns booming, these battleships cutting through heavy seas introduced a new and imposing tool to be used in competition for sea power.

Years before these battleships were built,

merchant ships with iron plating had been constructed. They were propelled by steam using paddlewheels or propellers. Steamships were also fitted with sails at first. In May 1854 the construction of the *Great Eastern* was begun in England. When this giant, 692 feet long and 82.7 feet wide, was completed in 1858 she could carry 4,000 passengers, a crew of 400 and a cargo of 6,000 tons. She was driven by steam using paddlewheels and propeller, and she also had six masts capable of carrying 58,000 square feet of sail.

The *Great Eastern* was more than twice as long and nearly twice as wide as the *Great Republic*. The iron ship traveled faster under steam (15 knots) than the speedy frigates under royal and skysail.

Just as the wooden ship was reaching its final stride, metal steamships were taking their first great steps forward. The four-, five- and seven-masted steel-hulled sailing ships of the early 1900s, many of them equipped with motors to raise and lower sail, work the pumps and heat the ship, fought a losing battle against such ships as the 790-foot-long *Mauretania*, launched in 1906, with 70,000 horsepower turbine engines.

With the introduction of safe and profitable steamships, the day of the great sailing ships came to an end. The age of sail is not over, however. Fishing, river and coastal trade is still carried on under sail in many parts of the world, and sailing as a sport or for recreation is as exciting as ever.

Great Eastern, *1858–1888*.

"The 790-foot-long Mauretania, *launched in 1906, with 70,000-horsepower turbine engines."*

Glossary

ABAFT	toward the stern.
ABEAM	at right angles to the line of the keel.
ADMIRAL	the commanding officer of a naval fleet. The term originated in the Near East, where an Ameer of the Sea was known as the *amir-al-bahr*.
AFT	toward the stern, or in the stern.
ALEE	away from the direction of the wind.
ALOFT	above the decks; in the masts or rigging; overhead.
ALTITUDE	the height of a heavenly body above the horizon. (2) The height above sea level.
AMIDSHIPS	along the keel. (2) In or toward the middle of a ship. (3) Midway between the ends.
ANTARCTIC	the south polar regions. At or near the South Pole.
ARCTIC	the north polar regions. At or near the North Pole.
ARMADA	a fleet of warships. (See *flotilla*.)
ARMING	the process of filling the recess at the bottom of a sounding lead with tallow or other soft substance to pick up sand, mud, etc.
ARTEMON MAST	an ancient spar serving as a foremast.
ASTERN	behind the vessel.
ASTROLABE	an instrument formerly used to take the altitude of the sun and the stars.
ASTRONOMICAL DAY	24 hours of solar time recorded from noon to noon. The day begins at noon, called 0 hours, and runs through the 24 hours.
ATHWART	across, from side to side. (2) At right angles to the fore-and-aft line of a vessel.

ATOLL   a ring-shaped coral reef enclosing, or nearly enclosing, a lagoon.

AUSTRAL   southern. (The *Terra Australis* of the 1600s is now called Australia.)

AVAST   an order to stop, or hold; corrupted from the Dutch *hou'vast,* an order to hold fast.

AWEATHER   toward the direction of the wind.

AWEIGH   when the anchor has just broken free of the bottom.

BACKSTAY   rigging leading aft of the masthead to the sides or stern of a vessel to help support the mast.

BALLAST   any heavy substance placed in the lower hold of a vessel to increase stability. Brick, stone, sand, iron, gravel, and in modern ships water and other substances are used. A ship sails "in ballast" when it carries no cargo.

BANK   One of the original meanings was a long seat. The term applied to the bench occupied by rowers in a galley. (2) An arrangement of rowers in a line or rowers sitting behind or above one another in a line. (3) To double-bank the oars means to place two men at one oar. (4) A raised shelf of land in the sea where the water is relatively shallow, such as the fishing banks off Nova Scotia and Newfoundland. A *banker* would be a vessel that visits the offshore fishing banks.

BARGE   a luxuriously outfitted vessel of state. (2) A name for craft built for towage purposes, often flat-bottomed.

BATTEN   a thin strip of wood used to reproduce the curves of lines of a vessel's hull. (2) Long, thin strips of wood set in lateen sails to preserve the shape. (3) Battens are strips of wood or iron that fit over the staples in the hatch coamings and secure the tarpaulins. When securely wedged the hatches are said to be *battened down.* A ship is said to be *battened down* when all hatches and openings have been fastened before proceeding to sea.

BEAKHEAD   a structure projecting forward from the stem, under the bowsprit. Often decked and surrounded by rails, it gave the bows of sailing ships their characteristic appearance until early in the 1800s.

BEAM   the width of a vessel. (2) One of the horizontal transverse timbers holding a ship together (athwartship timber on which the deck is laid). (3) The midpoint of the sides. (4) A vessel may be referred to as a four-beam vessel; that is, its length is four times its beam. Clipper ships were from five to six times their beam in length.

BEAR A HAND   to help, to hurry work. An order to a passing seaman "to bear a hand there" would be an order to pitch in and help the work along.

BEARING	the direction of an object at sea expressed in terms of compass points or degrees. (2) To *bear down* on another vessel would be to approach it from windward. (3) To *bear off* is to push a boat away from a wharf or ship's side.
BEATING	working to windward by successive tacks.
BEFORE THE MAST	men living in the forecastle. As used in the title of Richard Henry Dana's book *Two Years Before the Mast,* it meant Dana had been a crew member living in the forecastle for two years.
BELAY	to make a rope fast.
BELAYING PIN	a bar of wood or metal, set in the pin rails, for securing the running rigging. (Sometimes in whaling vessels they were made of whalebone.)
BELAY THERE	Stop!
BILGE	the curve of the hull below the waterline. (2) The lowest internal part of the hull. Bilge water collects at this point by seepage. (3) To damage, or stave, a vessel's bottom. (4) A bilge well is a well into which bilge water drains to be pumped away.
BINNACLE	a box for holding the compass. (2) A stand of wood used to house the compass.
BOAT	a small craft: one that can be hoisted onto a vessel. River craft, no matter what size, are usually called boats.
BONAVENTURE	the outer mizzen, the fourth mast aft.
BONNET	a strip of canvas laced to the foot of a sail to catch more wind.
BOOM	the spar to which the foot of a sail is secured.
BOW	the forward part of a vessel.
BOWSPRIT	the heavy spar projecting forward from the bow.
BROADSIDE	the side of a vessel above the water. (2) The simultaneous firing of all guns on one side of a warship.
BULKHEAD	the upright partitions that form cabins or other separate compartments on a ship.
BULWARK	the side of a vessel that extends above the level of the deck. (2) The railing which runs along the sides of a vessel.
BURDEN (burthen)	the carrying capacity of a vessel.
CALIBER	the diameter of the bore of a gun. (The bore is the hole made by boring.) (2) The diameter of a bullet, cannonball, etc.
CARVEL	edge-to-edge planking for a vessel's hull. A carvel-built vessel is smooth-sided.

CAULK	to fill the seams of a ship with oakum or cotton to prevent leaking.
CHANTY	a song sung to unify the men working; composed for various kinds of heavy work to give the men a steady tread or heave.
CHART	a map showing the sea and coastline details.
CHRONOMETER	A seagoing clock fitted with gimbals to offset the motion of the vessel, it has a variable lever and a compensated balance wheel. Used at sea to determine longitude. It is set at Greenwich Mean Time (G.M.T.) for purposes of navigation.
CIRCUMNAVIGATE	to sail around; used generally to mean around the world.
CLEAN	a term applied to a vessel's lines. If they are fine at the ship's entrance and at the counter, going through the water without disturbing it unduly, the ship is said to be clean-lined.
CLINKER	planked so that one plank laps over the next. This is a light, strong method of planking.
COAMING	the raised structure around the edge of the hatches.
CONVOY	one or more ships sailing under the protection of an armed vessel.
COUNTER	the after part of a vessel's hull where the lines converge toward the stern.
CROSS STAFF	an instrument used in taking the altitude of heavenly bodies.
CUTWATER	the forward edge of the prow.
DEAD RECKONING	the position found by calculating the distance covered and course steered. The influences of current and wind are taken into account to determine the position of the ship at sea.
DECK	the flooring of a vessel. (The word *flooring* is used for convenience; see *floor*.)
DOUBLE-ENDED	with a stern somewhat similar to the bow. A simple example is a canoe.
ENSIGN	a flag of nationality carried at the stern. (2) The lowest commissioned naval rank.
ENTRANCE	that part of a vessel which cleaves the water, displacing it for its passage; the forward part, especially at the waterline and below.
ESCUTCHEON	the part of the vessel's stern ornamented with her name.
FAST	To make fast is to secure.
FATHOM	nautical depth measurement of six feet.
FENDER	Fenders come in many shapes and materials—rope, timber, cork, etc. They all serve to prevent chafing between

a ship and the wharf or between one ship and another.

FIGUREHEAD an ornamental figure that rides beneath the bowsprit.

FLAGSHIP the vessel carrying the commander of a fleet or squadron.

FLEET a sea force. (2) A number of ships sailing in company. (3) A large number of ships of a naval unit under the orders of an admiral.

FLOOR the bottom of the hull. (2) Any of a number of deep, transverse framing members at the bottom of a steel or iron hull.

FLUSH DECK an unbroken deck fore and aft, where no walls or erections extend across a vessel.

FLOTILLA a fleet, usually applied to small vessels.

FOOTROPE the rope hanging beneath the yard on which men stand while furling or reefing.

FORE toward the bow. (2) The foremast; its sails and rigging.

FORE AND AFT in line with the keel, lengthwise of the ship.

FORE-AND-AFT SAILS sails carried in a fore-and-aft direction.

FORECASTLE the raised deck at the bow. (2) The location of the crew's quarters.

FOREMAST the first mast aft the bow.

FORWARD toward the bow.

FOUNDER to fill and sink at sea.

FRAME the skeleton structure of a vessel.

FRAMING the skeleton structure that supports the planking and decks. It consists of frames, beams, keel, etc.

FULL-ENDED a vessel whose waterline section is well rounded at bow and stern.

FURL to roll up and secure sails on a yard or boom.

GALLERY a balcony built outside the body of a vessel.

GALLEY the kitchen of a ship. (Not to be confused with the type of ship called a galley.)

GEAR equipment.

GIMBALS a contrivance which permits an object mounted in or on it to tilt freely in any direction, in effect suspending the object so that it will remain horizontal even when its support is tipped.

GIVE the stretching of a new rope or the bending of a spar. (2) The give of a ship is the amount of yielding, or bending, to the forces of wind and water.

GRATINGS wooden or iron openwork covers for hatches, decks, etc.

GROUND A vessel grounds when it touches bottom.

GUNWALE (gunnel) the heavy top rail of a ship or boat.

HALF DECK the deck that runs aft from about the center of the vessel. (2) The afterpart of the gun deck on naval vessels.

(3) In some small vessels the deck extending over part of the vessel.

HALYARDS (halliards)   ropes or tackles for hoisting sails and yards.

HAND   a crew member.

HATCH   an opening in the deck of a ship.

HAUL   to pull. A long pull is a heave.

HEADSAILS   the sails forward of the foremast, fore-and-aft type, often called jibs.

HEAVE   To heave away is to take a long pull. (2) To throw. (3) Heave ahead is to move forward by taking in a line. (4) To heave to is to stop. This is done by bringing a ship to the wind, shortening and trimming sails so that the ship lies almost motionless in the water but always heads up out of the trough.

HEEL   the leaning over of a ship in heavy seas or wind. (2) The after part of the keel at the sternpost. (3) The inner end of a bowsprit or jib-boom. (4) The foot of a mast.

HELM   the tiller or wheel.

HELMSMAN   the man who steers the ship at sea. (See *pilot*.)

HIGH SEAS   that part of the ocean where no nation has jurisdiction.

HOGGED   a term applied to a vessel whose bow and stern have drooped, while the midsection of the ship humps up like the back of a hog. (See *sagged*.)

HOLD   the cargo space in the hull of a vessel. (2) The large lower compartment of a vessel used for cargo.

HOLE   variation of *hold*.

HOOKER   a colloquial expression given to an old vessel.

HOUSING OF A MAST   that part of the mast belowdecks.

HULK   a large ship often associated with the carrack. (2) A ship. (3) An unseaworthy old vessel, often used as a storeship or prison.

ICEBERG   an enormous floating mass of ice. The portion rising out of water is small compared to the portion that is submerged.

IN A SHIP   People sail *in* a vessel just as they live *in* a house.

JETTISON   to heave cargo overboard to lighten a vessel in distress.

JIB   a triangular sail set forward of the foremast. Jibs as a group are called headsails.

JURY MAST   a temporary mast put up in place of one that has been broken or carried away. Jury anchor, jury rig, jury rudder, etc., are all makeshift items used on a damaged vessel.

KEEL   the backbone of a vessel on which the framework of the whole is built up. It is the lowest longitudinal timber of a vessel from which the frames or ribs, stem and sternpost rise.

KEELSON (kelson)   a secondary keel lying above the main keel, to which it is bolted.

KID   a tub or pan in which the forecastle rations are carried.

KNEES   right-angled strengthening and supporting pieces of timber.

KNOT   one nautical mile per hour—a measure of speed, not distance.

LABOR   the heavy straining of a vessel.

LACING   the line that secures the sail to the spar.

LANDFALL   the sight of or coming to land.

LANDMARK   a conspicuous or prominent object on land that helps establish a ship's position.

LASH   to secure by binding closely.

LATEEN   a triangular sail set from a yard at an angle of about 45 degrees to the mast.

LEAGUE   a unit of distance. The American and English marine league is equal to about three nautical miles.

LEEBOARD   a heavy frame of plank on the side of shallow-draught vessels to prevent the vessel from making leeway.

LEE SIDE   away from the direction of the wind.

LEEWARD   toward the wind.

LEEWAY   the sideward drift of a vessel from her course to leeward.

LENGTH BETWEEN PERPENDICULARS   the distance measured from the forepart of the stem to the afterpart of the stern.

LENGTH OVERALL   the distance from the foremost part of the stem to the aftermost part of the stern.

LINE   small rope. The use of the word rope was avoided at sea, and still is; almost all ropes were lines.

LINE OF BATTLE   the formation known technically as line ahead in which all the heavy ships are grouped in line, one following another, to be in movement together in battle.

LINES OF A VESSEL   a set of scale drawings defining the hull. It is made up of three plans: a body plan, a half-breadth plan, and a sheer plan. Called lines plan or lines drawing.

LIST   the leaning of a vessel due to greater weight on one side.

LOG   any of the various instruments used to determine the speed of the vessel.

LOGBOOK   a record of events on board a ship.

LOOSE-FOOTED   a fore-and-aft sail not laced to, or without, a boom.

MADE OR BUILT MAST   one constructed of several pieces of wood banded together into a round spar.

MAGAZINE   a compartment for the storage of ammunition.

MAIN DECK   in a cargo ship the part of the upper deck that lies between the poop and the forecastle. (2) In a naval vessel the deck that runs the full distance fore and aft and is usually just below a complete upper deck.

MAINMAST   the second mast from the bow.

MAINSAIL   the square sail set from the main yard. The lowest and often the principal sail on the mainmast. It is also called the main course. The three principal sails from the deck upward are the mainsail, the topsail and the topgallant sail.

MAKE   to attain, to make to a harbor. (2) Make fast is to secure. (3) Make sail is to set sail.

MAKING   The sea is "making" when it begins to rough up, usually before a storm.

MAN   To man is to put the number of hands to work that a job requires.

MAN THE YARDS   to stand men from yardarms to mast as a salute. (See *yard, yardarms*.)

MAN-OF-WAR   an armed vessel.

MARINER   an old expression used to denote a man with experience at sea. (It is used today to denote a Master-Mariner, or as in the poem by Coleridge called *The Ancient Mariner*.)

MARITIME   of the sea; connected with the sea.

MAROON   to put a person ashore at an isolated place with no means of leaving. A means of punishment.

MASTHEAD   the top of a mast.

MASTER   the commander of a merchant vessel.

MAST   an upright spar, usually carrying sails. The four principal masts on a ship, running from bow to stern, were: fore, main, mizzen, and bonaventure.

MERCHANTMAN   a commercial vessel.

MESS   a meal; a group of men eating together. (These men are called *messmates*.)

MIDSHIPS   the central fore-and-aft line of a vessel. Sometimes used when referring to the waist or middle of the fore-and-aft length. (Also, *amidships*.)

MILE   The length of the nautical sea mile varies from 6,046 feet at the equator to 6,109 feet at the Poles. In practical navigation, 6,080 feet is probably used by the majority of people, and when dealing with short distances 6,000 feet or 2,000 yards is used. The statute mile used on land is 5,280 feet.

MIZZEN   the third mast from the bow.

MODEL   a small reproduction of a vessel.

MOLD (mould)   a pattern of a certain part of a vessel.

MOLD LOFT	a loft where the pattern of a vessel is laid out.
NAUTICAL	relating to ships and navigation.
NAVAL	pertaining to warships, the navy.
NAVIGATE	to direct a ship on its course.
OAKUM	a caulking material made aboard ship from odds and ends of used rope. Today caulking is made commercially.
OARLOCK	a device to hold the oar when in use, usually made with forked jaws and a shank that is set in the gunwale of a boat.
OCEAN CURRENT	consistent movement of water in the open ocean.
OCEANOGRAPHY	the branch of physical geography dealing with the ocean.
OLÉRON	The Laws of Oléron, based on Roman law and named after one of Richard I's commanders, were sea laws used in England in the 1200s. Later, the Laws of Oléron were enlarged on in France.
OPEN BOAT	an undecked boat.
ORLOP DECK	the lowest deck.
PILOT	the man who steers or guides a ship into or out of a harbor, or any place especially dangerous. In the Laws of Oléron a false and treacherous pilot was condemned to suffer the most unmerciful death.
PITCH	the fore-and-aft motion of a vessel.
PLANKS	the lengths of wood forming the outside skin and the decks and inner lining of a vessel.
PLOT	to put a vessel's course down on a chart.
POOP	a superstructure at the stern of a vessel. (2) The aftermost part of a vessel. (3) The deck abaft the mizzen in a flush-decked three-masted vessel. (4) The raised deck and afterstructure at the stern of a vessel.
PORT	the left side of a vessel when looking toward the bow (at one time called the *larboard* side).
PORTHOLES	openings in the vessel's side for light and air and for guns.
QUARTERDECK	usually the space abaft the gangway to the mizzenmast. However, the quarterdeck on a naval vessel is clearly defined by the commanding officer. In ancient vessels with high poops the deck began at a point a quarter of the length from the vessel's stern.
QUAY	a loading and discharging place for vessels.
RAKE	the inclination of the mast in the fore-and-aft line from vertical, or the angle that the overhang of the stem or stern takes with the perpendicular.
RAM	the projecting portion of the lower stem on naval vessels.
RATE	the class in which a naval vessel belongs.

RATLINE	the lines fastened crosswise to the shrouds of a vessel which are used as steps to go up and down the rigging.
REEF	to reduce a sail area.
REEF POINTS	short pieces of rope set in the reefbands (reinforcing strips of canvas) of a sail.
RIBS	the frames of a vessel.
RIG	the arrangement of masts, sails, etc., on a vessel. (2) To put in proper order for working use.
RIGGING	the ropes of a vessel.
ROLL	the movement of a vessel from side to side.
RUDDER	a paddle, oar, or broad, flat piece of wood at the vessel's stern used for steering.
SAGGED	the downward slope of a vessel toward the middle; the opposite of hogged.
SAILS	pieces of canvas, papyrus, etc., set from masts, yards, booms, etc., which are used to catch the wind that propels a vessel forward.
SANDGLASS	an hourglass.
SEA ANCHOR	a drag used to help a vessel ride in greater safety during stormy weather.
SEA WATER	weighs 64 pounds to the cubic foot, while fresh water weighs 62½ pounds and river water about 63.
SECURE	to make fast or firm.
SEXTANT	an astronomical instrument used for measuring angular distances, especially the altitude of the sun, moon and stars at sea.
SHAKEDOWN CRUISE	a cruise intended to prepare a new vessel for regular service. It helps familiarize the crew with the features and peculiarities of the vessel; it also "breaks in" the vessel, pointing up its good and bad features.
SHEATHING	the metal sheets covering a vessel's bottom.
SHEER	the upward curve of the deck. (2) A sudden change in course.
SHEET	a line used to control a sail.
SHIP	a square-rigged vessel with three or more masts.
SHIP-OF-THE-LINE	a warship with enough guns to fight in the line of battle.
SHROUDS	lines going from the top of the mast to the sides of a vessel, to help support the mast.
SICK BAY	the quarters set aside on a ship for use as a hospital or dispensary.
SKIN	the inside or outside of a vessel's planking.
SOUNDINGS	the action of sounding or finding the depth of water by the use of line and lead. (2) A vessel is *on soundings* when

the bottom can be reached with the deep-sea lead, and
off soundings when it cannot.

SPAR DECK   the upper deck of a flush-decked vessel.

SPARS   the term applied to all masts, yards, booms, etc.

SPRIT   a light spar crossing a fore-and-aft sail diagonally from the mast to the upper aftermost corner, serving to extend the sail. (2) See *bowsprit*.

SPRITSAIL   the sail attached to a yard slung under the bowsprit.

SQUARE SAILS   nearly rectangular-shaped sails. All four sides need not be of equal length. More often than not the top and bottom, or head and foot, of a sail are longer than the sides, or leech. Also, the head is often shorter than the foot. From earliest times, in English, the term *square* has been applied to anything having an approximately square form.

STARBOARD   the right side of a vessel when looking toward the bow.

STAVE   to break planking inward.

STAY   a piece of rigging that supports a mast from forward. (See *backstay, shrouds*.) To stay is to support.

STAYSAIL   a triangular fore-and-aft sail set from various stays.

STEERING OAR   a long, broad oar used as a rudder.

STEM   the curved upright timber at the bow of a vessel.

STERN   the afterpart of a vessel.

STERNPOST   a more or less upright timber that rises from the afterend of the keel and supports the rudder.

STOVE   broken inward. (See *stave*.)

STUDDING SAILS   light sails set from removable extensions of the yardarms. (See *square sails*.)

THWARTS   In early ships these were the planks or timbers running from one side of the ship to the other side. They were above the deck, and oarsmen used them as seats. If you have ever been in a rowboat the seat you sat on was probably a thwart. (2) Across.

TILLER   a bar of wood connected to the rudder head in a horizontal position. The tiller acts as a lever by which the rudder is moved and the ship steered. (See *wheel, whipstaff*.)

TOPGALLANT SAIL   the square sail above the topsail. (See *topsail, mainsail*.)

TOP-HAMPER   all spars and gear above the ship's deck.

TOPSAIL   the sail above the mainsail. (See *mainsail*.)

TRAJECTORY   the course followed by a projectile shot from a gun.

TRAMP   a vessel that goes wherever freight is obtainable. Such a vessel does not travel established and regular runs.

TRANSOM STERN   a stern that is flat above the waterline.

TUMBLE HOME   the degree to which the sides of a vessel veer from the perpendicular.

UNRIG	to take down the rigging.
UNSHIP	to detach or remove anything from its working place, for example, to unship a mast, oar, etc.
VESSEL	a floating structure of any kind that is a seagoing craft, or the larger river and lake craft.
VOYAGE	a long journey by water. (2) A trip by sea in which a return is made to the starting point.
WAIST	the middle part of the fore-and-aft line. (2) That part of a vessel's deck between the forecastle and the quarter-deck.
WALE	the thick outside planking on the sides of a vessel. Wales are broader and thicker timbers than the rest, and extend horizontally, at different heights, from stem to stern. They are used to brace and strengthen the hull.
WATCH	a seaman's assigned duty period.
WATERLINE	the part of the outside of a ship's hull that is just at the water level. (2) Any one of certain structural lines of a ship, parallel with the surface of the water, that represent the contour of the hull at various heights above the keel.
WEIGH	to raise the anchor.
WHEEL	the steering wheel attached by means of ropes and pulleys to the tiller. (See *whipstaff, tiller*.)
WHIPSTAFF	a handle attached to the tiller used as a lever to control the steering of a vessel. (See *tiller*.)
WORKING SAILS	those used regularly.
YARD	a spar crossing a mast horizontally from which a square sail is set.
YARDARM	A yard is divided into two parts, port and starboard; the outer quarter of each of these parts is the yardarm.
YAW	to deviate temporarily from a straight course. (2) To steer badly.
YEOMAN	a petty officer in a navy whose duties deal with clerking or storekeeping.

Bibliography

ABELL, SIR WESCOTT. *The Shipwright's Trade.* Cambridge University Press, 1948.
A delightful book, although a good deal has been learned about ancient boat building since 1948.

ACKERKNECHT, E. H. *History and Geography of the Most Important Diseases.* Hafner Publishing, Co., Inc., 1965.
Dr. Ackerknecht's history of scurvy and other diseases is a wonderful work.

ALBION, R. G. *Forests and Sea Power.* Harvard University Press, 1926.
Extremely interesting history of the use of timber in shipbuilding.

ALBION, R. G. *Exploration and Discovery.* The Macmillan Co., 1965.

ALDEN, C. S., and Earle, R. *Makers of Naval Tradition.* Ginn & Co., 1925.
The naval careers of John Paul Jones and Thomas Macdonough, among others.

ANDERSON, R. and R. C. *The Sailing Ship.* W. W. Norton & Co., Inc., 1926.
An interesting and readable book that has been revised a number of times.

ANDREWS, K. R. *Drake's Voyages—A Re-assessment of Their Place in Elizabethan Maritime Expansion.* Charles Scribner's Sons, 1967.
A book of adventure filled with many surprising details about sailors and ships in the time of Queen Elizabeth I.

ANDREWS, K. R. *Elizabethan Privateering; English Privateering During the Spanish War 1585-1603.* Cambridge University Press, 1964.
Presents a clear picture of an often little understood subject.

ARCHIBALD, E. H. H. *The Wooden Fighting Ship.* Blandford Press, 1968.
Lively and interesting.

ARMSTRONG, R. *The Merchantmen.* Frederick A. Praeger, 1969.
A history of wooden cargo-carriers, especially those connected with the East India Company in England.

ASTON, M. *The Fifteenth Century: The Prospect of Europe.* Harcourt, Brace & World, Inc., 1968.
A comprehensive and clear history so well written that it brings little known people from the past to life and makes the fifteenth century seem like yesterday.

133

Bibliography

134 AYMAR, BRANDT. *A Pictorial Treasure of Marine Museums of the World.* Crown Publishing, Inc., 1967.
  A pictorial guidebook to the maritime collections of the world.

BAKER, WILLIAM A. *Colonial Vessels.* Barre Publishing Co., 1962.
  Mr. Baker clearly enjoys his subject, and so will you.

BAKER, WILLIAM A. *Sloops and Shallops.* Barre Publishing Co., 1966.
  This is a complete work, and a good one.

BARJOT, ADMIRAL, and SAVANT, J. *History of Shipping.* Translated from the French by Carol Tomkins. Librairie Hachette, 1961.
  A large book illustrated with many colorful prints.

BATHE, B. W. *Ship Models.* Her Majesty's Stationery Office, 1963.
  Photographs and short histories of the models give a good idea of ships from earliest times.

BOWEN, F. C. *Wooden Walls in Action.* Halton & Co. Ltd., 1951.

BOWEN, F. C. *Conquest of the Sea.* Travel Publishing, 1940.

BOWERS, J. Z. *Western Medical Pioneers in Feudal Japan.* The Johns Hopkins Press, 1970.
  If you want to learn about doctors, sailors, or merchants from Holland, Spain, or Portugal in feudal Japan, this is the book to reach for.

BREASTED, J. H. *Ancient Times, A History of the Early World.* Ginn & Co., 1935.
  An excellent book, revised from the 1916 edition and since revised again.

BREWINGTON, M. V. *Chesapeake Bay Sailing Craft.* The Anthoensen Press, 1966.
  The illustrations alone—by Louis Feuchter—make this an exceptional book.

CALAHAN, H. A. *The Sky and the Sailor—A History of Celestial Navigation.* Harper & Brothers, 1952.

CANBY, COURTLANDT. *A History of Ships and Seafaring.* Hawthorn Books, Inc., 1965.

CAPPER, D. P. *Famous Sailing Ships of the World.* Frederick Muller, 1957.

CARLETTI, FRANCESCO. *My Voyage Around the World.* Translated by H. Weinstock. Pantheon Books, 1964.
  Written in the early 1600s by a merchant who in seeking profit found adventure.

CARPENTER, R. *The National Geographic Magazine: Everyday Life in Ancient Times: Highlights of the Beginnings of Western Civilization in Mesopotamia, Egypt, Greece & Rome.* The National Geographic Magazine, 1964.
  Published from articles appearing in the *National Geographic,* a magazine that is diligent about detail. The accuracy of the lively illustrations and information is a wonder.

CARPENTER, R. *Beyond the Pillars of Hercules.* Delacorte Press, 1966.
  Exploration at sea in ancient times.

CARSE, R. *The Twilight of Sailing Ships.* Grosset & Dunlap, 1965.

CARSON, RACHEL. *The Sea Around Us.* Oxford University Press, 1951.
  For anyone who wants to learn about the sea and its mysteries.

CASSON, L. *The Ancient Mariners.* The Macmillan Co., 1959.

CASSON, L. *History of Ships and Boats.* Doubleday, 1964.
  A colorful story told with a light and interesting touch.

CHAMBERLIN, E. R. *Early Life in Renaissance Times.* B. T. Batsford Ltd., 1965.

CHAPELLE, H. *United States National Museum Bulletin 219.* The National Watercraft Collection. United States Government Printing Office, 1960.

CHAPELLE, H. *The Baltimore Clipper*. The Marine Research Society, 1930.
The development of the Baltimore Clipper.

CHAPELLE, H., and POLLAND, L. *The Constellation Question*. Smithsonian Institution Press, 1970.
Mr. Chapelle argues that the present-day *Constellation* is a ship built in the 1850s. The second section of the book contains Mr. Polland's convincing rebuttal.

CLARK, A. H. *The Clipper Ship Era 1843-1869*. 7C's Press, Inc., 1970.

COWBURN, P. *The Warship in History*. The Macmillan Co., 1965.

COXERE, EDWARD. *Adventures by Sea of Edward Coxere 1647-1685*. Oxford University Press, 1946.
The story of a seaman and his life aboard ship and on shore in the 1600s.

CULVEN, HENRY B. *The Book of Old Ships*. Doubleday, Doran & Co., Inc., 1924.
An enjoyable and informative book.

DANA, R. H. *Two Years Before the Mast*. The Modern Library, 1936.
The best way to learn about life at sea in years past is through Dana and other writers who have actually lived a sailor's life. This book originally appeared in 1840, and it is full of information on how his ship was sailed, what the men did and said, and what life in the forecastle of a ship of the early 1800s was like.

DARWIN, CHARLES. *The Voyage of the Beagle*. The Natural History Library. Doubleday & Co., Inc., 1962.
The story of Darwin's amazing voyage originally appeared in the 1800s. It is well worth reading if you are interested in things nautical or in scientific investigation and discovery.

DEACON, General Editor. *Seas, Maps, and Men*. Doubleday & Co., Inc.. 1962.

DEABY, H. A. *Greek Coins*. Argonaut, Inc., 1967.

DE LA VARENDE, J. *Cherish the Sea*. Translated by M. Savill. Viking Press, 1956.

DEMARGRE, P. *Aegean Art*. Thames & Hudson, 1964.

DENIEUL-CORMIER, A. *A Time of Glory, the Renaissance in France*. Doubleday & Co., 1968.

DERRY, T. K., and WILLIAMS, T. I. *A Short History of Technology*. Oxford University Press, 1960.

DORN, W. L. *The Rise of Modern Europe*. Harper & Row, Publishers, 1940.

ELLIS, C. H. *Ships*. Hulton Press, 1957.

ERGANG, R. *The Renaissance*. D. Van Nostrand Co., Inc., 1967.

EVANS, E. *British Polar Explorers*. Collins, 1943.
The story of polar exploration by Frobisher, Hudson, and others told in brief form.

FARBROTHER, R., Editor. *Ships*. Paul Hamlyn Ltd., 1963.

FERRIS, R. G. *Explorers and Settlers*. U.S. Department of the Interior, 1968.
The story of the explorers and settlers of America told in such a clear and well-balanced way that many of the exploits will seem new and more interesting than before. The Hudson Valley, Florida, the Carolinas and many other areas not very often discussed in other books are included. Photographs, maps and illustrations help the reader get to know early America.

FOWLER, E. W. *English Sea Power in the Early Tudor Period, 1485-1558*. Cornell University Press, 1965.

FRANŹEN, A. *The Warship Vasa*. Norstedt & Bonnier, Publisher, 1960.

FRIEDLÄNDER, L. *Roman Life and Manners Under the Early Empire*, Vol. 1. Barnes & Noble, Inc. 1907.
Revised a number of times, this work gives detailed information about the period.

Bibliography

136 GARRISON, J. H. *Behold Me Once More*. Edited by W. M. Merrill. Houghton Mifflin Co., 1954.

This is a sad true story of life aboard ship in the 1800s. Garrison is a good storyteller who doesn't pull his punches.

GOLDOLPHIN, F., Editor. *The Greek Historians*. Random House, 1942.

HAMPTON, T. A. *The Sailor's World*. David and Charles Newton Abbot, 1968.

A good deal of information about sailing ships and how the wind sails them.

HANSEN, H. J., General Editor. *Art and the Seafarer*. Translated by J. and I. Moore. The Viking Press, 1968.

This book is filled with lovely prints and paintings of sailing ships of the 1700s and 1800s. It was first printed in the Federal Republic of Germany in 1966.

HAY, DENYS. *Europe in the 14th and 15th Century*. Longmans, 1966.

HEAD, B. V. *Guide to the Principal Gold & Silver Coins of the Ancients*. Argonaut Press, 1968.

HERMAN, ZVI. *Peoples, Seas and Ships*. Translated by Len Ortzen. Phoenix House, 1966.

A lively book about early ships and seamen.

HIGGINS, R. *Minoan and Mycenaen Art*. Frederick A. Praeger, Publishers, 1967.

HOLLAND, R. S. *Historic Ships*. Macrae, Smith Co., Publishers, 1926.

HOLMES, U. J., JR. *Daily Living in the 12th Century Based on the Observations of Alexander Neckam in London and Paris*. The University of Wisconsin Press, 1952.

When you are learning about the 1300s you will probably read a number of books with references to Alexander Neckam. Here are Alexander Neckam's original words, explained and enlarged upon in a clear way.

HOURANI, GEORGE FADLO. *Arab Seafaring in the Indian Ocean in Ancient and Early Medieval Times*. Princeton University Press, 1951.

The story of Arab seafaring told in a concise yet comprehensive way. Your only objection to this book may be that it could have been longer. It is a fascinating subject; the Arabs were great seamen.

HOYT, R. S. *Europe in the Middle Ages*. Revised edition. Harcourt, Brace & World, Inc., 1966.

HUYGHE, R., General Editor. *Larousse Encyclopedia of Prehistoric and Ancient Art*. Prometheus Press, 1967.

HUYGHE, R., General Editor. *Larousse Encyclopedia of Byzantine and Medieval Art*. Prometheus Press, 1963.

JONES, GWYN. *The Norse Atlantic Saga*. Oxford University Press, 1964.

This is a particularly interesting book about Norsemen.

JONES, TOM B. *Ancient Civilization*. Revised edition. Rand McNally & Co., 1968.

JOWETT, B. *Thucydides*. A translation. 2nd edition revised. The Clarendon Press, 1900.

KNIGHT, F. *The Sea Story*. The Macmillan Co., 1958.

A very well done book that makes the early explorations read like newspaper stories.

LANDSTROM, BJORN. *The Ship—An Illustrated History*. Doubleday & Co., Inc., 1961.

A large and colorful book. The artist's work is finely detailed and beautifully done.

LAING, ALEXANDER. *American Sail—A Pictorial History*. E. P. Dutton & Co., Inc., 1961.

LANE, FREDERIC C. *Venetian Ships & Shipbuilding During the Renaissance*. The Johns Hopkins Press, 1934.

A wonderfully detailed account of ships and trade in Venice.

LANE, FREDERIC C. *Venice and History, The Collected Papers of Frederic C. Lane.* The Johns Hopkins Press, 1966.
A somewhat advanced book, but in it the author has many interesting observations; for example, "The technical study of the shaping and rigging of ships is alone insufficient to make understandable the development and disappearance of different types."

LEWIS, MICHAEL. *The Navy in Transition 1814-1864.* Hodder & Stoughton, 1965.

LINDSAY, J. *The Ancient World, Manners & Morals.* G. P. Putnam's Sons, 1968.
A good account of seamen, wholesalers, retailers and others involved in overseas trade.

LINDSAY, NORMAN. *Ship Models.* Angus & Robertson, 1966.

LLOYD, C. *Ships and Seamen.* World, 1961.

LOVETTE, LELAND P. *Naval Customs, Traditions & Usage.* United States Naval Institute, 1939.
Naval history told without sanctimoniousness. There is everything in this book, from a history of naval expressions, to old and sometimes amusing naval customs on land and at sea. The book has been revised many times.

LUBBOCK, B. *Adventures by Sea from Art of Old Time.* The Studio Ltd., 1925.

MANUCY, ALBERT. *Artillery Through the Ages.* National Park Service Interpretive Series History No. 3. United States Government Printing Office. Reprint Edition, 1962.
A good history of the development of cannon.

MARCUS, G. J. *A Naval History of England.* Little, Brown & Co., 1961.

MARSDEN, WILLIAM. *The Travels of Marco Polo, the Venetian.* Edited and revised by Manuel Komroff. The Modern Library, 1930.

MARTINEZ-HIDALGO, J. M. *Columbus' Ships.* Barre Publishers, 1966.
The author uses Spanish sources which have not been used before and comes up with an interesting story.

MATTINGLY, GARRETT. *The Armada.* Houghton Mifflin Co., 1959.

MCPARR, C. *So Noble a Captain, Life and Time of Ferdinand Magellan.* Thomas Y. Crowell Co., 1953.
Magellan and his men are stimulating people to live with for a while.

MEIGGS, R. *Roman Ostia.* The Clarendon Press, 1960.

MELVILLE, HERMAN. *Moby Dick.* The Modern Library, 1950 edition.
Over a hundred years ago Herman Melville wrote this story about his experiences at sea on a whaling vessel.

MILLER, R. C. *The Sea.* Random House, 1966.

MITCHELL, H. *Ships That Made U.S. History.* Whittlesey House–McGraw-Hill Book Co., 1950.

MORISON, S. E. *The Oxford History of the American People.* Oxford University Press, 1965.
A wonderful and "human" history. The kind of book you can read and reread and still find exciting.

NEEDHAM, J. *Science and Civilization in China,* Vol. 1. Cambridge University Press, 1954.

NIMS, C. F. *Thebes of the Pharaohs.* Stein & Day, 1965.

NUSSBAUM, FREDERICK L. *The Triumph of Science and Reason, 1660-1685.* Harper & Brothers, Publishers, 1953.

OBER, F. A. *John and Sebastian Cabot.* Harper & Brothers, 1908.

OXENSTIERNA, E. G. *The World of the Norsemen.* Translated by J. Sondheimer. Weidenfeld & Nicolson, 1967.

138 PARKMAN, F. *La Salle and the Discovery of the Great West.* The New American Library of World Literature, 1962.

This work was first published in 1869: an exciting event in the story of history books. Little, Brown & Company of Boston first brought it out; since then many editions have appeared, and with good reason. It's a real adventure story and an excellent historical study at the same time.

PARR, CHARLES M. *Jan Huygen van Linschoten: 1563-1611, The Dutch Marco Polo,* Vol. 2, Age of Discovery Trilogy. T. Y. Crowell Co., 1964.

PARRY, J. H., General Editor. *The Establishment of European Hegemony.* Harper, 1961.

PARRY, J. H., Editor. *The European Reconnaissance, Selected Documents.* Harper, 1968.

PENDLEBURY, J. *The Archaeology of Crete.* Biblo & Tannen, 1963.

PETERSON, M. *History Under the Sea.* Smithsonian Institution Press, Reprint Edition, 1969.

A wonderful book about underwater exploration. How nails, wood, and items such as clay pipes and ballast are used to determine the age and nationality of shipwrecks of galleons and other types of old vessels.

PINNEY, R. *Underwater Archaeology: Treasures Beneath the Sea.* Hawthorn Books, Inc., 1970.

The subject of underwater archaeology presented in a simple manner. The author tells of many explorations, including the Danish National Museum's excavations in the Roskilde Fiord.

POLLAND, L., and CHAPELLE, H. *The Constellation Question.* Smithsonian Institution, 1970. See Chapelle.

POOL, L. and G. *Danger! Icebergs Ahead!* Random House, 1961.

A primer on icebergs. Although simply written, it tells an informative story.

QUENNELL, M. and C. *A History of Everyday Things in England 1066/1499.* B. T. Butsford Ltd., 1931.

RACKL, HANNS-WOLF. *Diving into the Past.* Translated by R. J. Floyd. Charles Scribner's Sons, 1968.

RAWLINGS, G. B. *Ancient, Medieval, Modern Coins.* Ammon Press, 1966.

ROGERS, S. *The Sailing Ship—A Study in Beauty.* Harper & Brothers, Publishers, 1950.

ROUTH, C. R. N. *They Saw It Happen in Europe 1450-1600.* Basil Blackwell, 1965.

ROWE, W. H. *The Maritime History of Maine.* The Bond Wheelwright Co., reprinted by W. W. Norton & Co., Inc., 1967.

SANDERLIN, G. *Across the Ocean Sea, A Journal of Columbus's Voyage.* Harper & Row, Publishers, 1966.

SCHÄUFFELEN, OTMAR. *Great Sailing Ships.* Frederick A. Praeger, 1969.

An illustrated catalogue and history of 150 extant barks, barkentines, brigs, brigantines, frigates, schooners and other large sailing vessels built since 1628.

SCHURZ, WILLIAM LYTLE. *The Manila Galleon.* E. P. Dutton & Co., Inc., 1939; republished 1959.

SEDILLOT, R. *A Bird's-Eye View of French History.* Translated by G. Hopkins. Geo. G. Harrap & Co., Ltd., 1952.

SEYMOUR, T. D. *Life in the Homeric Age.* Biblo & Tannen, 1963.

SHARP, A. *The Voyages of Abel Janszoon Tasman.* Oxford University Press, 1968.

SIMPSON, JACQUELINE. *Everyday Life in the Viking Age.* B. T. Batsford Ltd., 1967.

The equipment of warriors and their ships and travels, all nicely told and illustrated.

SJØVOLD, THORLEIF. *The Oseberg Find and Other Viking Ship Finds.* Translated by M. Fjeld. Universitetets Oldsaksamling, 1963.

Southworth, J. *The Ancient Fleets, The Story of Naval Warfare Under Oars 2600 B.C.–1597 A.D.* Wayne Publishers, Inc., 1968.

Southworth, J. *The Age of Sail, The Story of Naval Warfare Under Sail 1213 A.D.–1853 A.D.* Wayne Publishers, Inc., 1968.

Stevers, M., and Pendlebury, J. *Sea Lanes, Man's Conquest of the Ocean.* Minton, Balch & Co., 1935.

Many interesting stories about the sea.

Starr, Chester G. *The Roman Imperial Navy 31 B.C.–324 A.D.* Barnes & Noble, Inc., 1960.

Starr has examined poetry, writing, tombstones, etc. to reconstruct the history of the Roman navy.

Svensson, S. *Sails Through the Centuries.* The Macmillan Co., 1962.

Swain, Joseph Ward. *The Ancient World.* 3 vols. Harper & Row, Publishers, 1950.

Taylour, Lord William. *The Mycenaeans.* Frederick A. Praeger, 1964.

Throckmorton, Peter. *Ship Wrecks and Archaeology.* Little, Brown & Co., 1969-70.

A young man's thrilling adventures underwater, told in an exciting and clear way.

Torr, C. *Ancient Ships.* Argonaut, Inc., 1964.

The building, docking and sailing of ancient ships explained in detail.

Tucker. *Life in the Roman World of Nero and St. Paul.* The Macmillan Co., 1936.

Tunis, E. *Oars, Sails and Steam.* The World Publishing Co., 1952.

A well-balanced book with delightful illustrations. The descriptions of ships are brief but interesting.

Tunstall, Brian. *The Realities of Naval History.* George Allen & Unwin Ltd., 1936.

van Loon, H. W. *The Golden Book of Dutch Navigators.* The Century Co., 1916.

Villiers, A. J. *Ships Through the Ages—A Saga of the Sea. National Geographic,* Vol. 123, pp. 469-545, April 1963.

The author of this article has written many enjoyable studies connected with the sea. The *National Geographic* magazine can always be counted on to publish delightful works in this field, not only to look at, but to read.

Walker, Ernest P. *Mammals of the World.* 3 vols. The Johns Hopkins Press, 1964.

Wallbank and Taylor. *Civilizations Past and Present,* Vols. 1 and 2. Revised edition. Scott Foresman & Co., 1949.

Whipple, A. *Yankee Whalers in the South Seas.* Doubleday & Co., Inc., 1954.

Whitlark, F. L. *Introduction to the Lakes.* Greenwich Book Publishers, 1959.

Wilson, D. *The Vikings and Their Origins: Scandinavia in the First Millennium.* Thames & Hudson, 1970.

A pleasant history of the early Vikings, their early houses, ships and art.

Woldering, I. *Gods, Men and Pharaohs.* Harry N. Abrams, Inc., 1967.

Woodrooffe, T. *Vantage at Sea.* St. Martins Press, 1958.

The Spanish Armada and the details of the expedition of Spain against England in the 1500s. Very readable and interesting.

Wroth, L. C. *The Way of a Ship.* The Southworth-Anthoensen Press, 1937.

Ziauddin, Alavi S. M. *Geography in the Middle Ages.* Sterling Publishers, 1966.

Index